Penguin Education

Penguin Modern Management Texts
General Editor: D. S. Pugh

Writers on Organizations
D. S. Pugh, D. J. Hickson and C. R. Hinings

Writers on Organizations
Second Edition

D. S. Pugh, D. J. Hickson and C. R. Hinings

Penguin Books

Penguin Books Ltd, Harmondsworth,
Middlesex, England
Penguin Books Inc., 7110 Ambassador Road,
Baltimore, Md 21207, U.S.A.
Penguin Books Australia Ltd,
Ringwood, Victoria, Australia

First published by Hutchinson 1964
Second edition published by Penguin Books 1971
Copyright © D. S. Pugh, D. J. Hickson and C. R. Hinings, 1964, 1971

Made and printed in Great Britain by
Hazell Watson & Viney Ltd,
Aylesbury, Bucks
Set in Monotype Times Roman

Penguin Modern Management Texts

This volume is one of a series of unit texts designed, in conjunction with the Penguin Modern Management Readings, to cover the field of management studies in a comprehensive but flexible way. The short unit texts, at an attractive price to the student, may be thought of as 'building bricks' which may be used by both teacher and student in combination with other books to build up the particular teaching programme. In each of the component subject areas of management studies, an area editor, who is a leading teacher in the field, has designed a series of titles covering aspects of his subject from many points of view. The teacher thus has flexibility in planning his course and in recommending texts for it. The pace at which developments are taking place in management thinking and practice requires the series to be adaptable. Our plan allows a unit to be revised, or a fresh unit to be added, with maximum speed and minimal cost to the reader.

The unit text approach also allows us to include many books which will take an innovative approach to a particular topic, as well as those more conventional in their treatment. The international range of authorship will, in addition, bring out the richness and diversity of the subject, and encourage the reader to share in its intellectual excitement.

D.S.P.

*To our parents and to
our professional father-figures*

Contents

Foreword

There comes a time when the serious student is drawn more and more into the history of his subject as its challenge unfolds. There may be disappointments in the process but there are compensations of greater weight. There is the revelation of first principles in the making, the crystallizing of thinking and, above all, the stimulus to the reader's own pursuit of knowledge.

The student of management has a harder lot than some of his fellows. The worthwhile thinking is difficult to identify. There has been insufficient time yet for the best writing to be distilled. To cover the ground, the student would have to spend more time than he is usually prepared or able to give. This indeed is the problem at the Administrative Staff College, Henley-on-Thames. To meet it we invited D. S. Pugh, D. J. Hickson and C. R. Hinings to write this book.

I like to think of it as a guide-book. Much is to be learned from its perusal. And it invites the reader in a spirit of inquiry to make at least a few journeys to the sources themselves, armed with some knowledge.

It would have been easy but dull for the authors to have chosen the well-trodden path of biographies and summaries. Instead, they have elected to focus their attention on various aspects of organizations and to submit the contributions which thirty-three past and present writers have made in terms of the structure, functioning and management of organizations, people in organizations and the organization in society. A highly readable text is the result. It is also a measure of the authors' achievement, deriving as it does from an intimate knowledge of the literature and considerable skill in presentation.

The book makes no pretence to be comprehensive, but with clear understanding of the students' predicament, the authors offer a coherent introduction to some of the most valuable work which has been accomplished in this field.

The first edition of this book, published in 1964, served its purpose well, but it was substantially shorter than the present volume. Brevity is essential for the audience we have in mind, but we were, during the past six years at the Administrative Staff College, in the specially favoured position of being able to take the opinions of over a thousand experienced managers who were readers of the first edition, and it became clear that a more substantial volume would be even more valuable. I believe that this second edition in the Penguin Modern Management series will be not only a vade-mecum for succeeding generations of Henley members, but also an essential possession for many others who are interested in the study of organizations and their management. I am very glad that a companion volume, *Organization Theory: Selected Readings*, is in course of preparation.

J. P. Martin-Bates
Principal, Administrative Staff College, Henley-on-Thames

Introduction

It is a commonplace of discussions among administrators and managers to hear that all organizations are different. Frequently the implication is that there can be little in common between them and consequently no coherent description of organizations. Even so, administrators continue to forgather to discuss their problems in a way which suggests that, after all, they find they have common interests and value each other's experience and advice.

Even if all organizations are indeed different it is possible to state these differences and to classify them, so that something useful can be said about various kinds of organizations and the ways in which they function. In this book we have presented a synopsis of the work of a number of leading writers who have attempted this analysis. These authors have a variety of different backgrounds. Some are drawing upon their experience as practising managers, some on their knowledge of local and national government administration, some on the findings of their research work. All are modern in that the influence of their work has been felt within the last fifty years. All have attempted to draw together information and distil theories of how organizations function and how they should be managed.

Their writings have been theoretical in the sense that they have tried to discover generalizations applicable to all organizations. Every act of an administrator rests on assumptions about what has happened and conjectures about what will happen; that is to say, it rests on theory. Theory and practice are inseparable.

We have divided the book into five chapters each concerned with a different aspect of organizations. We do not purport to have included everything that can be said on the subject, but to have selected a number of topics which complement one another. The complexities of relationships created by the coming together of numbers of people form a variety of organization structures – Chapter 1 of the book. There are a variety of ways of analysing the managerial and other activities which together may be thought of as the functioning of organizations – Chapter 2. There is always the problem of their administration or management – Chapter 3. The proliferation of viewpoints and theories about the reactions of people in organizations is represented by just a handful of well-known names – Chapter 4. Finally, there is the place of organizations in the wider trends of contemporary societies – Chapter 5.

Each writer has been allocated to a particular chapter according to what we consider to be his main impact. This, of course, is a considerable oversimplification, although we hope a useful one – particularly for those coming new to this field, or having read little in it. It is for them that this book is intended. But it must be stressed that the division into sections is artificial, made specifically for the purposes of this exposition. There is much overlapping between the various aspects treated in the different chapters, and many writers have made contributions which might be placed in more than one chapter.

Our object has been to give a direct exposition of the author's views. We have not essayed critical analysis which would be a quite different task. It is our hope that the reader will bring his own critical appraisal to each writer. Even so, we are extremely conscious of the very considerable selection and compression which is involved in presenting a man's work in a few pages. Some distortions must inevitably result. We can only plead the best of intentions in that our hope is to entice the reader to go to the originals in their richness and complexity.

We are grateful to J. P. Martin-Bates who, in sponsoring this volume for the Administrative Staff College, Henley-on-Thames, gave us every encouragement. Morris Brodie not only acted as the link between ourselves and the College but gave generously of constructive comment and criticism. Our colleague Tom Lupton read the manuscript and made a number of helpful suggestions. We also wish to thank Miss Mildred Wilhelm for her many hours spent in typing the manuscript and our colleagues in the Industrial Administration Research Unit for their forbearance. The arduous task of compiling the index was ably undertaken by Miss C. Brookes. Our wives, as always, suffered most in the cause.

I. A. Research Unit
Birmingham College of
Advanced Technology
1963

The demand for a second edition of this book has given us the opportunity of revising a considerable proportion of the essays included, and of bringing them up-to-date where necessary. We have also added descriptions of the work of a further nine writers on the subject. Our aim in this revision and expansion has remained the same: to present a concise introductory account of each writer's contribution in order to give a general overview of the field, and to attract the reader to follow his initial interest by going to the original sources, which as before are fully listed. Simultaneously with the publication of this edition, a companion volume, *Organizations: Selected Readings*, edited by D. S. Pugh is being issued. This brings together in convenient form extracts from the work of several of the writers summarized here.

We are grateful to the Faculty of Business Administration of the University of Alberta, and to our colleagues there, for providing the occasion of our meeting to complete this revision.

Organizational Behavior Research Unit
University of Alberta
1970

1 The Structure of Organizations

The decisive reason for the advance of bureaucratic organization has always been its purely technical superiority over any other form of organization.

Max Weber

It would be entirely premature, then, to assume that bureaucracies maintain themselves solely because of their efficiency.

Alvin W. Gouldner

Most organizations most of the time cannot rely on their participants to carry out their assignments voluntarily.

Amitai Etzioni

The danger lies in the tendency to teach the principles of administration as though they were scientific laws, when they are really little more than administrative expedients found to work well in certain circumstances but never tested in any systematic way.

Joan Woodward

The beginning of administrative wisdom is the awareness that there is no one optimum type of management system.

Tom Burns

When a new technology is introduced an inappropriate form of work organization – that associated with the technical trial of the machinery – tends to be carried over to subsequent operational units.

Eric Trist

All organizations have to make provision for continuing activities directed towards the achievement of given aims. Regularities in activities such as task allocation, supervision and coordination are developed. Such regularities constitute the organization's structure and the fact that these activities can be arranged in various ways means that organizations can have differing structures. Indeed, in some respects every organization is unique. But many writers have examined a variety of structures to see if any general principles can be extracted. This variety, moreover, may be related to variations in such factors as the objectives of the organization, its size, ownership, geographical location and technology of manufacture, which produce the characteristic differences in structure of a bank, a hospital, a mass production factory or a local government department.

Three of the writers in this section are primarily concerned with postulating a classification of different types of organizational structure, and three with the factors which produce particular structures. Max Weber outlines three different types of organization by examining the bases for wielding authority. Alvin W. Gouldner starts from one of Weber's types, bureaucracy, and shows that even in one organization, three variants of this type can be found. Amitai Etzioni examines the basis on which various types of organization obtain the 'compliance' of their members. Joan Woodward has studied the relationship between production systems, technology and structure in manufacturing concerns. She demonstrates that the technology is a major determinant of the structure. Tom Burns is concerned with the impact of changing technology, and the attempts of old established firms to adjust to new situations. Eric Trist and his colleagues at the Tavistock Institute demonstrate the utility of regarding organizations as interdependent 'socio-technical' systems.

All the contributors to this chapter suggest that an appropriate structure is vital to the efficiency of an organization and must be the subject of careful study in its own right.

Max Weber

Max Weber (1864–1920) was born in Germany. He qualified in law and then became a member of the staff of Berlin University. He remained an academic for the rest of his life, having a primary interest in the broad sweep of the historical development of civilizations through studies of the sociology of religion and the sociology of economic life. In his approach to both of these topics he showed a tremendous range in examining the major world religions such as Judaism, Christianity and Buddhism, and in tracing the pattern of economic development from pre-feudal times. These two interests were combined in his classic studies of the impact of Protestant beliefs on the development of capitalism in Western Europe and the USA. Weber had the prodigious output and ponderous style typical of German philosophers, but those of his writings which have been translated into English have established him as a major figure in sociology.

Weber's principal contribution to the study of organizations was his theory of authority structures which led him to characterize organizations in terms of the authority relations within them. This stemmed from a basic concern with why individuals obeyed commands, why people do as they are told. To deal with this problem Weber made a distinction between *power*, the ability to force people to obey, regardless of their resistance, and *authority*, where orders are voluntarily obeyed by those receiving them. Under an authority system, those in the subordinate role see the issuing of directives by those in the superordinate role as legitimate. Weber distinguished between organizational types according to the way in which authority is legitimized. He outlined three pure types which he labelled 'charismatic', 'traditional', and 'rational–legal', each of which is expressed in a particular administrative apparatus or organization. These pure types are distinctions which are useful for analysing organizations, although any real organization may be a combination of them.

The first mode of exercising authority is based on the personal qualities of the leader. Weber used the Greek term *charisma* to mean any quality of the individual's personality by virtue of which he is set apart from ordinary men and treated as endowed with supernatural, superhuman or at least specifically exceptional powers or qualities. This is the position of the prophet, messiah or political leader, whose organization consists of himself and a set of disciples: the disciples have the job of mediating between the leader and the masses. The typical case of this kind is a small scale revolutionary movement either religious or political in form, but many organizations have had 'charismatic' founders, such as Lord Nuffield (Morris Motors) and Henry Ford. However, as the basis of authority is in the characteristics of one person and commands are based on his inspiration, this type of organization has a built-in instability. The question of succession always arises when the leader dies and the authority has to be passed on. Typically, in political and religious organizations the movement splits with the various disciples claiming to be the 'true' heirs to the charismatic leader. Thus the process is usually one of fission. The tendencies towards this kind of breakdown can be seen in the jockeying for position of Hitler's lieutenants, Himmler and Göring, during the first few months of 1945. It exemplifies the problem of an heir to the leader, and even if the leader himself nominates his successor, he will not necessarily be accepted. It is unlikely that another charismatic leader will present himself; and so the organization must lose its charismatic form, becoming one of the two remaining types. If the succession becomes hereditary, the organization becomes traditional in form; if the succession is determined by rules a bureaucratic organization develops.

The bases of order and authority in *traditional* organizations are precedent and usage. The rights and expectations of various groups are established in terms of taking what has always happened as sacred; the great arbiter in such a system is custom. The leader in such a system has authority by virtue of the status that he has inherited, and the extent of his authority is fixed by custom. When charisma is traditionalized by making its transmission hereditary, it becomes part of the role of the leader rather than being part of his personality. The actual organizational form under a traditional authority system can take one of two patterns. There is the *patrimonial* form where officials are personal servants, dependent on the leader for remuneration. Under the *feudal* form the officials have much more autonomy with their own sources of income and a traditional relationship of loyalty towards the leader. The feudal system has a material basis of tithes, fiefs and beneficiaries all resting on past usage and a system of customary rights and duties. Although Weber's examples are historical his insight is equally applicable to modern organizations. Managerial positions are often handed down from father to son as firms establish their own dynasties based on hereditary transmission. Selection and appointment may be based on kinship rather than expertise. Similarly, ways of doing things in many organizations are justified in terms of always having been done that way *as a reason in itself*, rather than on the basis of a rational analysis.

The concept of rational analysis leads to Weber's third type of authority system, the rational–legal one, with its bureaucratic organizational form. This, Weber sees as the dominant institution of modern society. The system is called rational because the means are expressly designed to achieve certain specific goals, i.e. the organization is like a well-designed machine with a certain function to perform, and every part of the machine contributes to the attainment of maximum performance of that function. It is legal because authority is exercised by means of a system of rules and procedures through the office which an individual occupies at a particular time. For such organization Weber uses the name 'bureaucracy'. In common usage, bureaucracy is synonymous with inefficiency, an emphasis on red tape, and excessive writing and recording. Specifically, it is identified with inefficient public administration. But in terms of his own definition Weber states that a bureaucratic organization is technically the most efficient form of organization possible. 'Precision, speed, unambiguity, knowledge of files, continuity, discretion, unity, strict subordination, reduction of friction and of material and personal costs – these are raised to the optimum point in the strictly bureaucratic administration.' Weber himself uses the machine analogy when he says that the bureaucracy is like a modern machine, while other organizational forms are like non-mechanical methods of production.

The reason for the efficiency of the bureaucracy lies in its organizational form. As the means used are those which will best achieve the stated ends, it is unencumbered by the personal whims of the leader or by traditional procedures which are no longer applicable. This is because bureaucracies represent the final stage in depersonalization. In such organizations there is a series of officials, each of whose roles is circumscribed by a written definition of his authority. These offices are arranged in a hierarchy, each successive step embracing all those beneath it. There is a set of rules and procedures within which every possible contingency is theoretically provided for. There is a 'bureau' for the safe keeping of all written records and files, it being an important part of the rationality of the system that information is written down. A clear separation is made between personal and business affairs, bolstered by a contractual method of appointment in terms of technical qualifications for office. In such an organization authority is based in the office and commands are obeyed because the rules state that it is within the competence of a particular office to issue such commands. Also important is the stress on the appointment of experts. One of the signs of a developing bureaucracy is the growth of professional managers and an increase in the number of specialist experts with their own departments.

For Weber, this adds up to a highly efficient system of coordination and control. The rationality of the organization shows in its ability to 'calculate' the consequences of its action. Because of the hierarchy of authority and the system of rules, control of the actions of individuals in the organization is assured; this is the depersonalization. Because of the employment of experts who have their specific areas of responsibility and the use of files, there is an amalgamation of the best available knowledge and a record of past behaviour of the organization. This enables predictions to be made about future events. The organization has rationality: 'the methodical attainment of a definitely given and practical end by means of an increasingly precise calculation of means'.

This is where the link between Weber's interest in religion and organizations occurs. Capitalism as an economic system is based on the rational long-term calculation of economic gain. Initially for this to happen, as well as the expansion of world markets, a particular moral outlook is needed. Weber saw this as being supplied by the Protestant religion after the Reformation with its emphasis on this world and the need for individuals to show their salvation through their industry on earth. Thus, economic activity gradually became labelled as a positive good rather than as a negative evil. Capitalism was launched on its path, and this path was cleared most easily through the organizational form of bureaucracy which supplied the apparatus for putting economic rationality into practice. Providing as it does efficiency and regularity, bureaucratic administration is a necessity for any long-term economic calculation. So with increasing industrialization, bureaucracy becomes the dominant method of organizing, and so potent is it that it becomes characteristic of other areas of society such as education, government, politics, etc. Finally, the bureaucratic organization becomes typical of all the institutions of modern society.

Most studies of the formal, structural characteristics of organizations over the past two decades have started from the work of Max Weber. His importance lies in having made the first attempt to produce systematic categories for organizational analysis.

Bibliography

The Protestant Ethic and the Spirit of Capitalism, Allen & Unwin, 1930.

The Theory of Social and Economic Organization, Free Press, 1947.

GERTH, H. H., and MILLS, C. W. (eds.), *From Max Weber: Essays in Sociology,* Routledge & Kegan Paul, 1948.

Alvin W. Gouldner

Alvin W. Gouldner is an American sociologist currently working at Washington University, St Louis. He has conducted research into social problems for the American Jewish Committee and the Social Science Research Council. His initial research work was on industrial organizations, and he has been a consultant to the Standard Oil Company of New Jersey. He is currently interested in the application of social theory to social policy.

Gouldner has applied Weber's concepts (see p. 21) of bureaucracy and its functioning to modern industrial organizations. Weber's analysis was based on the assumption that the members of an organization will in fact comply with the rules and obey orders. He asked on what basis do the rule-promulgators and the order-givers obtain their legitimate authority. He gave no attention to the problem of establishing the legitimacy of authority, in the face of opposition and a refusal to consent on the part of the governed. This is a situation frequently met, for example, when a bureaucratic authority attempts to supplant a traditionalistic one, or when the rule of the expert or the rational–legal wielder of power is faced with resistance.

On the basis of a very close study of this type of situation in an American gypsum mine, Gouldner has described the effects of the introduction of bureaucratic organization in the face of opposition. The previous management system of the mine was based on 'the indulgency pattern'. The rules were ignored or applied very leniently; the men were infrequently checked on and were always given a second chance if infringements came to light. There was a very relaxed atmosphere and a favourable attitude of the workers to the company. Into this situation came the new mine manager who set about seeing that the rules were enforced, that the authority structure functioned effectively, and in general that an efficient rational–legal organization was operated. But this also resulted in a great drop in morale and increased management–worker conflict – including a wildcat strike.

In his analysis of this situation Gouldner was able to distinguish three patterns of bureaucratic behaviour: mock, representative and punishment-centred – each with its characteristic values and conflicts.

In *mock bureaucracy* the rules are imposed on the group by some outside agency, for example, a rule laid down by an insurance company forbidding smoking in a shop or official returns required outside the organization on the activities of members. Neither superiors nor subordinates identify themselves with or participate in the establishment of the rules, nor do they regard them as legitimate. Thus the rules are not enforced, and both superiors and subordinates obtain status by violating them. Smoking is allowed unless an outside inspector is present; purely formal returns are made, giving no indication of the real state of affairs. The actual position differs very much from the official position and people may spend a lot of time 'going through the motions'. This behaviour pattern of mock bureaucracy corresponds with the common conception of bureaucratic 'red tape' administration which is divorced from reality. However, in such a system, as Gouldner points out, morale may be very high since the informal values and attitudes of all participants are bolstered by the joint violation or evasion of the rules in order to get on with 'the real job'.

In *representative bureaucracy* Gouldner takes up and develops one strand of Weber's concept, the situation in which rules are promulgated by 'experts' whose authority is acceptable to all the members of the organization. Superiors and subordinates support the rules which fit in with their values and confer status on those who conform. For example, pressure may come from both management and workers to develop a safety programme; a high quality of workmanship may be expected and achieved. In this situation rules are enforced by superiors and obeyed by subordinates, perhaps with some tension but with little overt conflict. As the values are held in common by all, deviations are explained by well-intentioned carelessness or ignorance, since it would not be thought possible that the values are disputed. The joint support for the rules is buttressed by feelings of solidarity and participation in a joint enterprise. This behaviour pattern of representative bureaucracy corresponds very closely to the ideal forms of organization strongly advocated by such writers as Taylor and Follett (see pp. 97–101 and pp. 102–4) in which authority is based not on position but on accepted knowledge and expertise.

In the third type of bureaucracy, *punishment-centred*, the rules arise in response to the pressures *either* of management *or* workers. The attempt is made to coerce the other side into compliance. For example, management may introduce stricter control on production, clocking-in procedures and fines. This type of bureaucracy emphasizes the elements of authority and command – hierarchy in Weber's concept – although, as Gouldner points out, there can be a power struggle in which the solidarity of the subordinates imposes rules on the management, e.g. job demarcation rules, overtime bans, rigid redundancy procedures. Either superiors or subordinates consider the rules legitimate, and if conformity leads to a gain in status for one side this involves a loss in status for the other. Deviation from the rules is not explained away as in representative bureaucracy, but is regarded as wilful disobedience. Such a situation clearly entails much conflict and tension.

The patterns of behaviour characteristic of these three 'types of bureaucracy' may coexist in different degrees in any one organization, and they are perhaps better described as 'modes of bureaucratic functioning'. The punishment-centred mode, which is the most frequently used, is intended to produce an efficient organization working in conformity to rationally designed rules and procedures. It emphasizes the use of general and impersonal rules, which decrease the emphasis on the personal power of those in authority. This in turn leads to a reduction in interpersonal tension which promotes efficiency and reinforces the use of impersonal bureaucratic rules. This is the strength of bureaucracy – as Weber pointed out.

But Gouldner maintains that there are unanticipated consequences of bureaucratic functioning which Weber left out of account. General and impersonal rules, by their very nature, define what is *not* allowed and thus increase people's knowledge of what is the minimum acceptable behaviour, which tends to become the standard behaviour. This lowers efficiency and, in a punishment-centred bureaucracy, leads to increased closeness of supervision to see that the rules are carried out, and as a consequence to increased emphasis on authority and greater interpersonal tension. This results in the continued issue of formal impersonal rules to deal with the conflicts, and the cycle then begins again. Thus both the anticipated and unanticipated consequences of bureaucracy lead to a reinforcement of bureaucratic behaviour. The system is essentially unstable, achieving its goals only at the cost of much interpersonal tension and conflict.

Thus, rules have both positive and negative effects, anticipated and unanticipated consequences. An overall aim of rules is to overcome the effect of close supervision which makes power differences too visible and thereby may offend norms of equality. So rules serve as an equivalent for direct orders by providing a statement of the obligations of a particular job (their explicational function). However, in certain circumstances the informal group may provide this function, thereby leading to unanticipated consequences of conflict. Rules also provide an impersonal way of using authority (their screening function). Along with this, rules enable control to take place at a distance (their remote control function). But here again, the distance may get too great leading to a 'mock' situation of authority. Rules also constitute a definition of expectation, together with sanctions for non-performance (their punishment-legitimating function). But rules also define minimal standards allowing individuals to work at low levels of commitment (their apathy preserving function). It is the different possibilities in the operation of rules which provide the dysfunctions of bureaucracy.

Gouldner has also been concerned to distinguish different outlooks among administrators and to show the effects these have upon their attitudes to their jobs, their employing organizations, their professions and their colleagues. This arises from a further criticism of Weber. Gouldner suggests that there is an inherent contradiction in bureaucracy between a system of authority based on the appointment of experts, and authority based on hierarchy and discipline. In the first case authority is legitimized because of superior knowledge; in the second it arises from the office held. This represents a particular incompatibility in those organizations which employ large numbers of professionals who may have more technical knowledge than their hierarchical superiors. Gouldner distinguishes two main categories of administrators: *cosmopolitans* and *locals*. Cosmopolitans are administrators with little loyalty to the organization, but much committed to their specialized skills. They have an extremely professional outlook. They think of themselves primarily as engineers or accountants, for instance. Locals are administrators with great loyalty to the organization, but with little commitment to specialized skills. They think of themselves as 'company men'. Although organizations wish to retain the loyalty of their personnel (and therefore, for example, to promote by seniority from within) they also have a basic rational orientation towards efficiency (which requires appointment by skill and competence from wherever it is obtainable). This built-in dilemma is another major cause of tension in the modern organization.

Bibliography

Patterns of Industrial Bureaucracy, Routledge & Kegan Paul, 1955.
Wildcat Strike, Routledge & Kegan Paul, 1955.
'Cosmopolitans and locals: towards an analysis of latent social roles', 1, *Admin. Sci. Q.*, 1957, vol. 1, no. 2, pp. 281–306.
'Organizational analysis', in R. K. Merton *et al.* (eds.), *Sociology Today*, Basic Books, 1958.

Amitai Etzioni

Amitai Etzioni is a sociologist at Columbia University, New York, having previously worked at the Hebrew University, Jerusalem, and the Berkeley campus of the University of California. He is currently working in the area of conflict and peace research, something which grew out of his organizational interests. His concern with fundamental sociological problems led him to examine organizations as promising research sites for their solution.

In his work he starts from the problem of social order, asking the question of why organizations, or other social entities, keep going. This is the problem of social control which has interested social philosophers since the days of Plato and which was put in its most pristine form by Hobbes. It is similar to the concern of Weber (p. 19), and for Etzioni too the question to be answered is 'why do people in organizations conform to the orders given to them and follow the standards of behaviour laid down for them?' This problem occurs in all social organizations from the family to the nation state, but Etzioni sees it as being particularly crucial in formal organizations. This is because organizations are designed as instruments. When one is formed, whether it be in government, business, education or recreation, it has a specific reason for existing, a goal or purpose; 'natural' social systems such as the family, or a community, are much more diverse in what they do and it is difficult to think of them having goals. But because organizations have this characteristic of attempting to reach a goal, it becomes important to 'measure' how well they are doing. The result is an emphasis on performance.

Organizations continuously review their performance and

will change their practices in the light of this. Organizations therefore face special problems of controlling the behaviour of their members, because they must make sure that behaviour is in line with the requirements of performance.

Etzioni starts from the proposition that organizations, like other social units, require compliance from their members. Because of their intensive concern with performance (and also in the modern world, their size), organizations cannot rely on compliance coming essentially from the fact that members are completely committed to the aims of the organization. Also they cannot rely on an informal control system based on one individual influencing another such as occurs in the family. Organizations have formal systems for controlling what goes on in them; they have rewards and penalties of a clear and specific kind to ensure compliance from their members.

Compliance in any organization is two sided. On the one hand it consists of the control structures that are employed; the organizational power and authority structure which attempt to ensure that obedience is obtained. This Etzioni calls the structural aspect since it is concerned with the formal organizational system and the kind of power that the organization uses to enforce compliance. As organizations cannot completely rely on their members to carry out orders perfectly, it is necessary to have a hierarchy of authority, to have supervisors: it is necessary to have job descriptions and specified procedures for doing things; it is necessary to have a division of labour. All of these are attempts to make the organization less dependent on the whims of individuals by controlling behaviour. The organization exercises its power by these bureaucratic means.

The second aspect of compliance is based on the extent to which members of the organization are committed to its aims and purposes. This is the motivational aspect and is expressed in the kind of involvement that the individual has with the organization that he belongs to. The more intensely an individual is involved in the organization the more likely he is to work towards the realization of its goals. Etzioni argues that the more employees are committed, the less formal control mechanisms are needed. These two aspects of compliance are then used to produce a typology of organizations.

Etzioni outlines three kinds of power according to which organizations can be classified. The classification is based on the different means used to ensure that members comply. He distinguishes between coercive power, remunerative or utilitarian power, and normative or identitive power. They are based on physical, material and symbolic means respectively.

Coercive power rests essentially on the (possible) application of physical force to make sure that members of an organization comply with orders. Thus, the ability to inflict physical pain or to cause death for non-compliance is the use of this kind of power. Examples of organizations using physical means to different degrees are concentration camps and custodial mental hospitals.

Remunerative or utilitarian power rests on the manipulation of material resources. The organizational member's compliance is enforced because the organization controls materials, such as money, which the member desires. Thus, a system of rewards based on wages and salaries constitutes this kind of power. Business organizations are typically based on remunerative control.

Normative or identitive power comes from the manipulation and allocation of symbols. Examples of pure symbols are love, affection, prestige which can be used to extract compliance from others. Etzioni suggests that alternative, and perhaps more eloquent names would be persuasive or suggestive power. He sees this kind of power as most often found in religious organizations, universities, voluntary associations.

These are ideas which are useful for making broad comparative analyses of organizations based on predominant characteristics. But not all organizations with the same general objectives have similar control structures. Etzioni suggests that labour unions can be based on any of the three; 'underworld' unions controlled by mobsters relying on coercion; 'business' unions offering members wage increases and better working conditions are essentially remunerative; and 'political' unions centred on ideologies, rely on normative power. Most organizations attempt to employ all three kinds of power, but will usually emphasize one kind of power and rely less on the other two. Often different means of control are emphasized for different participants in the organization. Members at the bottom of the organization are often more likely to be subject to coercive measures, whereas higher participants are more likely to be subject to normative power.

As with power, Etzioni suggests three kinds of involvement. The classification is based on a dimension of low to high involvement, and the types are labelled alienative, calculative, and moral. In essence, involvement in an organization can run from highly intensive negative feelings to highly positive feelings with mildly negative and mildly positive in between.

Alienative involvement is the intensely negative end, and denotes dissociation from the organization by the member. Convicts and prisoners of war are usually alienated from the organizations of which they are members. With calculative involvement the member's relationship to the organization has little intensity and thus can be either positive or negative in a mild way. This is typical of business relationships. Finally, moral involvement denotes a positive and favourable view of the organization which is very intense. It is found in the highly committed church member, the loyal party member, etc.

When examined together, the three kinds of power and the three kinds of involvement generate nine types of compliance relationship in the organization:

Kinds of power	Kinds of involvement		
	Alienative	Calculative	Moral
Coercive	1	2	3
Remunerative	4	5	6
Normative	7	8	9

Etzioni argues that a particular kind of power and a particular kind of involvement usually go together; thus the most common forms of compliance found in organizations are 1, 5 and

9. Coercive power produces alienative involvement, and vice versa; remunerative power and calculative involvement will be found together; and similarly normative power and moral involvement are congruent with one another.

Organizations which represent these three empirically dominant types are a prison with an emphasis on custody rather than rehabilitation, a factory, and a church respectively. The other six possibilities are incongruent in the sense that the power system does not fit the involvement of the members. The result will be strain and a shift in one of the bases of compliance. Etzioni suggests that organizations which have congruent compliance structures will be more effective than those which suffer the strain and tension of incongruent systems. This argues that business organizations function most effectively when they use remuneration rather than coercion or symbols as the basis of control. They need a system which is subject to ease of measurement and which can be clearly related to performance. Coercion (such as threats of dismissal) and normative control (such as appeals to loyalty) can only be used secondarily.

However, it should always be remembered that there are many outside factors which affect the kind of control structure that an organization can have. In the kinds of societies which produce many complex organizations the state monopolizes the use of force; and indeed we find that it is state run institutions, such as prisons, which use coercive power. Other organizations, e.g. business, are not allowed to. Similarly, general market conditions such as the extent of competition, or the presence of a labour pool will affect the extent to which the utiliarian control used by a business firm will veer towards the coercive or normative end of the spectrum. Also, the beliefs that the participants bring to the organizations of which they are members, and their personality makeups will affect the degree to which they recognize particular kinds of control as legitimate. Etzioni points out the differences in response between the USA of today and of two generations ago that would result from the same exercise in coercive power – for example, a teacher slapping a pupil. The changing belief system means that organizations have to change their compliance structures.

Overall, Etzioni is interested in laying the base for a wide-scale comparative analysis of organizations. As such he produces a conceptual framework which is applicable to all organizations and which emphasises similarities and differences between organizations in different institutional areas.

Bibliography

A Comparative Analysis of Complex Organizations, Free Press, 1961.
Modern Organizations, Prentice-Hall, 1964.
'Organizational control structure', in J. G. March (ed.), *Handbook of Organizations*, Rand McNally, 1965.

Joan Woodward

Joan Woodward is Professor of Industrial Sociology at the Imperial College of Science and Technology, University of London. Her first research was undertaken from the University of Liverpool, but she is best known for her subsequent work on technology as director of the Human Relations Research Unit at South-East Essex College of Technology, which her research group at Imperial College has continued. She is a prominent member of the Institute of Personnel Management, and founded the personnel management course at Oxford University.

From 1953 to 1957 Woodward led the South-East Essex research team in a survey of manufacturing organizations in that area (see Woodward, 1958; 1965). In all, one hundred firms participated; though the amount of information obtained on them varied from firm to firm, and the published information is therefore on smaller numbers. Firms ranged in size from a hundred employees to over a thousand, and some were the main establishments of their companies whilst others were branch factories. The survey was supplemented by intensive studies of selected firms.

Woodward does not use sweeping classifications of organizations by types (such as those suggested by Weber – charismatic, traditionalistic, bureaucratic – or by Burns – organismic, mechanic). Rather than attempt in this way to summate whole ranges of characteristics of organizations, she investigates specific features such as the number of levels of authority between top and bottom, the span of control or average number of subordinates of supervisors, the clarity or otherwise with which duties are defined, the amount of written communication, and the extent of division of functions among specialists.

Woodward finds that firms show considerable differences in features such as these. Foremen may have to supervise anything from a handful to eighty or ninety workers; the number of levels of management in production departments may be anywhere from two to eight; communication can be almost entirely verbal or largely written. Why should these differences occur?

Woodward's team compared firms of different sizes, and examined differences in historical background, without finding any answer. But when differences in technology were studied, relationships were seen with many organizational features. It is not claimed as a result that technology is the only influence upon a firm's organization nor that individual managers make no impression, but technology is a major factor.

Woodward finds that the objectives of a firm – what it wishes to make, and for what markets – determine the kind of technology it uses. For example, a firm building novel prototypes of electronic equipment could not do so by the techniques of mass production which dominate vehicle manufacture. Production systems differ in their degree of technical complexity, from unit (jobbing) and small batch production, through large batch and mass production to the most complex, namely process production.

These three broad categories are sub-divided into nine sub-categories of production systems (see Woodward, 1958, for an earlier slightly different version) from least to most complex:

Unit and small batch
1. Production of units to customers' requirements.
2. Production of prototypes.
3. Fabrication of large equipments in stages.
4. Production of small batches to customers' orders.

Large batch and mass production
5. Production of large batches.
6. Production of large batches on assembly lines.
7. Mass production.

Process production

8. Intermittent production of chemicals in multi-purpose plant.
9. Continuous flow production of liquids, gases and crystalline substances.

Some firms used more than one of these production systems and so were placed in additional 'combined system' categories. A distinguishing feature of process systems is that they manufacture products measured by dimensions of weight or volume (e.g. liquids) rather than those usually counted as series of integral units (e.g. numbers of vehicles or of packaged goods).

In general, the higher the category the more it is possible to exercise control over the manufacturing operations because performance can be pre-determined. In a continuous-flow plant such as chemical installation the equipment can be set for a given result; capacity and breakdown probabilities are known. But in batch production full capacity may not be known and even well-developed production control procedures represent a continual attempt to set fresh targets in the face of many uncertainties of day-to-day manufacture. In unit production of prototypes, for example, it is almost impossible to predict the results of development work.

These differences in technology account for many differences in organization structure. In process technologies where equipment does the job, taller hierarchies are found with longer lines of command, but managed through committees rather than by instruction down the line. Such hierarchies include more trained university graduates; and since the proportion of personnel working directly on production is low, the hierarchy of administrative and managerial personnel is a comparatively large proportion of total employees.

Despite the complex administrative hierarchy of specialist staff and control departments common in large batch and mass production technologies, these have shorter lines of command and proportionately fewer managers and clerks. Their salient characteristic is large numbers of direct production operatives.

Unit and small batch production typically has an even shorter hierarchy where no manager is very far from the production work itself. This relies relatively heavily upon the production personnel themselves without extensive administrative controls.

Some organization characteristics do not differ straight along the nine technology categories. On some, large batch and mass production is often distinctive whilst unit and process production have much in common with each other. The large numbers of semi-skilled workers on which mass production is based mean that the span of control of supervisors is very wide, and since results are obtained through the pressure exerted by bosses upon subordinates, human and industrial relations may be strained. Typical of both unit and process production are comparatively small groups of skilled workers with more personal relationships with their supervisors.

Similarly, the complex production control problems of large batch and mass systems are reflected in their numbers of staff specialists, greater paperwork, and attempted clear-cut definition of duties, leading to more mechanistic organizations as Burns (p. 44) has called them.

A rough assessment of the firms on both financial and market performance and on reputation showed that the apparently more successful firms had organizational characteristics near the median or average for their category of technology. Perhaps there is one form of organization most appropriate to each system of production. Successful process firms must have taller, more narrowly based, organization pyramids; successful unit production firms must have relatively short pyramids; and so on.

Certainly more prolonged case-studies carried out by Woodward and her colleagues to test out the results of the initial survey showed that a change of technology category seems to force changes in organization. This in itself may bring conflict among those whose interests are affected, especially if the change is into batch type production. Firms were studied which moved from unit to batch, attempts being made to rationalize and increase the scale of production; and from process to batch, where for example a firm began to package a product previously sold in bulk. In such cases, middle managers and supervisors find that in batch production their days disappear in a confusion of calls and contacts with other people, that this subjects them to greater personal stress, and that their responsibility for production overlaps with that of new planning and control departments.

Indeed, such changes in technology may alter the whole status of the several functions in a firm. This is because the cycle of manufacture places development, production and marketing in a different order in different technologies. In unit or jobbing systems, marketing precedes development and production follows last, since not until a customer requires a product and it is designed can production occur. In large batch and mass systems, the development and production of a new line precedes its mass marketing. In process systems, development of a possible product and marketing to assured customers must precede commitment of capital to special purpose plant to produce it. In each system, the most critical function is the central one which has the greatest effect on success. That is, in unit systems, development has most importance and status; in mass systems it is production; in process systems it is marketing.

Woodward and her colleagues have carried out further detailed case studies of managerial control in its various forms as the link between the technology of manufacture and organizational structure and behaviour. Reeves and Woodward, in a chapter in *Industrial Organization, Behaviour and Control*, focus upon two dimensions of managerial control systems: first, the extent to which control varies between being personal and impersonal; secondly, the degree to which control is fragmented.

Along the first dimension, there is a range of control systems from completely personal hierarchical control at one extreme, as operated by an owner-employer, to completely impersonal mechanical control at the other, as operated by measurement mechanisms and the automatic controls of machine tools. In the middle of the range come the impersonal control processes

which are based on administrative procedures, such as production planning and cost systems. Firms may be compared
along this dimension, which is associated with characteristic
effects upon structure and behaviour. The most important
effect is that movement towards impersonal control involves a
separation between the planning and execution stages of the
work process.

At the personal end of the scale there is almost total overlap
between planning and execution; with impersonal administrative control processes there is considerable separation but the
planning departments such as production control, quality
control and cost control are involved in the execution of the
work; at the mechanical end of the scale there can be total
separation – the control designers and planners not being
concerned at all with the operations since they have already
built in correction mechanisms at the planning stage. Indeed
the planning and design stages at the mechanical control end
of the scale may be the concern of a separate organization as
when a chemical engineering firm undertakes the design and
erection of a automated continuous-flow chemical plant
complete with mechanical control processes, which is then
handed over to the contracting organization.

The second dimension of control systems studied by Reeves
and Woodward was the extent to which control was fragmented, ranging from a single integrated system of control at
one extreme, to multi-system fragmented control at the other.
To obtain a single integrated system, a firm would continuously attempt to relate the standards set for various departments to the performance and adjustment mechanisms
associated with them. At the other end of the scale, a firm
might have a number of control criteria operating indepen-
dently which are continuously reconciled by the supervisor or
the production operative. A job has to be done by a particular
date as set by production control, to a particular standard as
set by quality control, to a cost limit as set by cost control, by
particular methods as set by work study, and so on. An inevitable result of having a multiplicity of systems with fragmented
control is conflict, when the supervisor attempts to satisfy

each of the control criteria and in doing so jeopardizes his performance on the others.

The two dimensions of control processes are used together to generate a four-fold typology of systems in a developmental sequence. Four categories are outlined:

1. Firms with unitary and mainly personal controls, such as an entrepreneurial firm, where the owner would himself relate time and quality to cost. This type is characteristic of unit and small batch production.

2. Firms with fragmented and mainly personal controls, such as a firm where more individuals were involved in setting control criteria.

3. Firms with fragmented and mainly impersonal administrative or mechanical controls, such as a firm where the control criteria are impersonally set by functional departments. Most large batch and mass production firms fall here or in category 2.

4. Firms with unitary and mainly impersonal administrative or mechanical controls, such as a firm controlling the total manufacturing process to a master plan, perhaps using a computer for information processing and process control. This type is characteristic of process production.

The basic assumption and conclusion of Woodward's work is that meaningful explanations of differences in organization and behaviour can be found in the work situation itself. The technology of this work situation should be a critical consideration in management practice. There is no one best way. She warns against accepting principles of administration as universally applicable. The same principles can produce different results in different circumstances; many principles derive from experience of large-batch or mass production only and are not likely to apply in other technologies. Careful study of the objectives and technology of a firm is required.

Woodward's study pioneered both in empirical investigation and in setting a fresh framework of thought. Prior to it, thinking about organization depended on the apt but often over-generalized statements of experienced managers, and on isolated case-studies of particular firms. Woodward showed the possibilities of comparisons of large numbers of firms so that generalizations might be securely based and their limits seen.

She forces thinking away from the abstract elaboration of principles of administration to an examination of the constraints placed on organization structure and management practice by differing technologies and their associated control systems.

Bibliography

The Dock Worker, Liverpool University Press, 1955.

'Management and technology', *Problems of Progress in Industry*, no. 3, HMSO, 1958.

The Saleswoman: A Study of Attitudes and Behaviour in Retail Distribution, Pitman, 1960.

Industrial Organization: Theory and Practice, Oxford University Press, 1965.

Industrial Organization: Behaviour and Control (ed.), Oxford University Press, 1970.

Tom Burns

Tom Burns is a contemporary British research worker who is Professor of Sociology in the University of Edinburgh. His early interests were in urban sociology and he worked with the West Midland Group on Post-war Reconstruction and Planning. Since going to Edinburgh he has been particularly concerned with studies of different types of organization and their effects on communication patterns and on the activities of managers. He has also explored the relevance of different forms of organization to changing conditions – in particular to the impact of technical innovation.

In collaboration with a psychologist (G. M. Stalker), Burns has studied the attempt to introduce electronics development work into traditional Scottish firms, with a view to their entering this modern and rapidly expanding industry as the markets for their own well-established products diminished. The difficulties which these firms faced in adjusting to the new situation of continuously changing technology and markets led him to describe two 'ideal types' of management organization which are the extreme points of a continuum along which most organizations can be placed.

The *mechanistic* type of organization is adapted to relatively stable conditions. In it the problems and tasks of management are broken down into specialisms within which each individual carries out his assigned, precisely defined, task. There is a clear hierarchy of control, and the responsibility for overall knowledge and coordination rests exclusively at the top of the hierarchy. Vertical communication and interaction (i.e. between superiors and subordinates) is emphasized, and there is an insistence on loyalty to the concern and obedience to superiors. This system corresponds quite closely to Weber's rational–legal bureaucracy (see p. 21).

The *organismic* (also called *organic*) type of organization is adapted to unstable conditions when new and unfamiliar problems continually arise which cannot be broken down and distributed among the existing specialist roles. There is therefore a continual adjustment and redefinition of individual tasks and the contributive rather than restrictive nature of specialist knowledge is emphasized. Interactions and communication (information and advice rather than orders) may occur at any level as required by the process, and a much higher degree of commitment to the aims of the organization as a whole is generated. In this system, organization charts laying down the exact functions and responsibilities of each individual are not found, and indeed their use may be explicitly rejected as hampering the efficient functioning of the organization.

The almost complete failure of the traditional Scottish firms to absorb electronics research and development engineers into their organizations leads Burns to doubt whether a mechanistic firm can consciously change to an organismic one. This is because the individual in a mechanistic organization is not only committed to the organization as a whole. He is also a member of a group or department with a stable career structure and with sectional interests in conflict with those of other groups. Thus there develop power struggles between established sections to obtain control of the new functions and resources. These divert the organization from purposive adaptation and allow out-of-date mechanistic structures to be perpetuated and 'pathological' systems to develop.

Pathological systems are attempts by mechanistic organizations to cope with new problems of change, innovation and uncertainty while sticking to the formal bureaucratic structure. Burns describes three of these typical reactions. In a mechanistic organization the normal procedure for dealing with a matter outside an individual's sphere of responsibility is to refer it to the appropriate specialist or, failing that, to a superior. In a rapidly changing situation the need for such consultations occurs frequently; and in many instances the superior has to put up the matter higher still. A heavy load of such decisions finds its way to the chief executive, and it soon becomes apparent that many decisions can only be made by going to the top. Thus there develops the *ambiguous figure system* of an official hierarchy and a non-officially-recognized system of pair relationships between the chief executive and some dozens of people at different positions below him in the management structure. The head of the concern is overloaded with work, and many senior managers whose status depends on the functioning of the formal system feel frustrated at being by-passed.

Some firms attempted to cope with the problems of communication by creating more branches of the bureaucratic hierarchy, e.g. contract managers, liaison officers. This leads to a system described as the *mechanistic jungle*, in which a new job or even a whole new department may be created, whose existence depends on the perpetuation of these difficulties. The third type of pathological response is the *super-personal* or *committee system*. The committee is the traditional way of dealing with temporary problems which cannot be solved within a single individual's role, without upsetting the balance of power. But as a permanent device it is inefficient, in that it has to compete with the loyalty demanded and career structure offered by the traditional departments. This system was tried only sporadically by the firms, since it was disliked as being typical of inefficient government administration; attempts to develop the committee as a super-person to fulfil a continuing function that no individual could carry out met with little success.

For a proper understanding of organizational functioning, Burns maintains, it is therefore always necessary to conceive of organizations as the simultaneous working of at least three social systems. The first of these is the formal authority system derived from the aims of the organization, its technology, its attempts to cope with its environment. This is the overt system in terms of which all discussion about decision-making takes place. But organizations are also cooperative systems of people who have career aspirations and a career structure, and who compete for advancement. Thus decisions taken in the overt structure inevitably affect the differential career prospects of the members, who will therefore evaluate them in terms of the career system as well as the formal system, and will react accordingly. This leads to the third system of relationships which is part of an organization – its political system. Every organization is the scene of 'political' activity in which individuals and departments compete and cooperate for power. Again all decisions in the overt system are evaluated for their relative impact on the power structure as well as for their contribution to the achievement of the organization's goals.

It is naïve to consider the organization as a unitary system equated with the formal system, and any change to be successful must be acceptable in terms of the career structure and the political structure as well. This is particularly so with modern technologically based organizations which contain qualified experts who have a career structure and a technical authority which goes far beyond the organization itself and its top management. Thus the attempt to change from a mechanistic to an organismic management structure has enormous implications for the career structure (which is much less dependent on the particular organization) and the power system (which is much more diffuse deriving from technical knowledge as much as formal position).

'A sense of the past and the very recent past is essential to anyone who is trying to perceive the here-and-now of industrial organization.' If the organizational structure is viewed as a resultant of a process of continuous development of the three social systems of formal organization, career structure and political system, a study of this process will help firms to avoid traps they would otherwise fall into. Adaptation to new and changing situations is not automatic. Indeed many factors militate against it, and amongst the most important is the existence of an organization structure appropriate to an earlier phase of industrial development.

Eric Trist
and the work of the Tavistock Institute

Eric Trist is a social psychologist who for over twenty years was the senior member of the Tavistock Institute of Human Relations, London. During that time he has, with a number of colleagues (including F. E. Emery and the late A. K. Rice) been conducting a programme of research and consultancy investigations into the structure and functioning of organizations from a 'systems' point of view. He is currently Professor of Organizational Behaviour and Ecology at the Wharton School of the University of Pennsylvania.

In collaboration with K. W. Bamforth (an ex-miner) Trist studied the effects of mechanization in British coal mining. With the advent of coal-cutters and mechanical conveyors, the degree of technical complexity of coal-getting was raised to a higher level. Mechanization made possible the working of a single long face in place of a series of short faces, but this technological change had a number of social and psychological consequences for the work organization and the worker's place in it, to which little thought was given before the change was introduced. The pattern of organization in short face working was based on a small artisan group of a skilled man and his mate, assisted by one or more labourers. The basic pattern around which the work relationships in the longwall method were organized is the coal face group of forty to fifty men, their shot-firer and 'deputies' (i.e. supervisors). Thus the basic unit in mining took on the characteristics in size and structure of a small factory department, and in doing so disrupted the traditional high degree of job autonomy and close work relationships with a number of deleterious effects.

The mass production character of the longwall method

necessitates a large scale mobile layout advancing along the seam, basic task specialization according to shift, and very specific job roles with different methods of payment within each shift. In these circumstances there are considerable problems of maintaining effective communications and good working relations between forty men spatially spread over two hundred yards in a tunnel, and temporally spread over twenty-four hours in three successive shifts. From the production engineering point of view it is possible to write an equation that 200 tons equals 40 men over 200 yards over 24 hours, but the psychological and social problems raised are of a new order when the work organization transcends the limits of the traditional, small face-to-face group undertaking the complete task itself. The social integration of the previous small groups having been disrupted by the new technology, and little attempt made to achieve any new integration, many symptoms of social stress occur. Informal cliques which develop to help each other out can only occur over small parts of the face, inevitably leaving some isolated; individuals react defensively using petty deceptions with regard to timekeeping and reporting of work; they compete for allocation to the best workplaces; there is mutual scapegoating across shifts, each blaming the other for inadequacies (since in the new system with its decreased autonomy, no one individual can normally be pinpointed with the blame, scapegoating of the absent shift becomes self perpetuating and resolves nothing). Absenteeism becomes a way of the miner compensating himself for the difficulties of the job.

This study of the effects of technological change led Trist to develop the concept of the working group as being neither a technical system nor a social system, but as an interdependent socio-technical system. The technological demands place limits on the type of work organization possible, but the work organization has social and psychological properties of its own that are independent of the technology. From this point of view it makes as little sense to regard social relationships as being determined by the technology as it does to regard the manner in which a job is performed as being determined by the social–psychological characteristics of the workers. The social and technical requirements are mutually interactive and they must also have economic validity, which is a third interdependent aspect. The attainment of optimum conditions for any one of these aspects does not necessarily result in optimum conditions for the system as a whole, since interference will occur if the others are inadequate. The optimization of the whole may well require a less than optimum state for each separate aspect.

In further studies of mining, Trist found that it was possible, within the same technological and economic constraints, to operate different systems of work organization with different social and psychological effects, thus underlining the considerable degree of organizational choice which is available to management to enable them to take account of the social and psychological aspects. A third form of operation known as the 'composite longwall method' was developed which enabled mining to benefit from the new technology while at the same time allowing some of the characteristics of the shortwall method to be continued. In the composite system, groups of men are responsible for the whole task, allocate themselves to shifts and to jobs within the shift, and are paid on a group bonus. Thus the problems of over-specialized work roles, segregation of tasks across shifts with consequent scapegoating and lack of group cohesion were overcome. For example, it became common for a sub-group that had finished its scheduled work for a shift before time, to carry on with the next activity in the sequence in order to help those men on the subsequent shift who were members of their group. The composite longwall method was quite comparable in technological terms with the conventional longwall method, but it led to greater productivity, lower cost, considerably less absenteeism and accidents, and greater work satisfaction, since it was a socio-technical system which was better geared to the workers' social and psychological needs for job autonomy and close working relationships.

This socio-technical system approach was also applied to supervisory roles by Rice in studies of an Indian textile firm.

He found that it was not enough to allocate to the supervisor a list of responsibilities (see Fayol, p. 61) and perhaps insist upon a particular style of handling men (see Likert, p. 146). The supervisor's problems arise from a need to control and coordinate a system of men–task relationships, and in particular to manage the 'boundary conditions', that is, those activities of this system which relate it to the larger system of which it is a part. In order to do this effectively, it is necessary to have an easily identifiable arrangement of tasks so that it is possible to maximize the autonomous responsibility of the group itself for its own internal control, thus freeing the supervisor for his primary task of boundary management.

In an automatic weaving shed for example, in which the occupational roles had remained unchanged since hand weaving, the activities of the shed were broken down into component tasks, with the number of workers required determined by work studies of the separate tasks. Those in different occupational tasks worked on different numbers of looms; weavers operated 24 or 32, battery fillers charged the batteries of 48, smash hands served 75, jobbers 112, the bobbin carrier 224, etc. This resulted in the shift manager having to interact about the job regularly with all the remaining 28 workers on his shift, jobbers having to interact with 14, smash hands with 9, a weaver with 7, etc., all on the basis of individual interactions aggregated together only at the level of the whole shift, with no stable internal group structure. Rice carried through a reorganization to create 4 work groups of 6 men, each with a group leader, each with an identifiable group task and a new set of interdependent work roles to carry it out. The boundaries of these groups were more easily delineated, and thus the work leader's task in their management facilitated. As a result there was a considerable and sustained improvement in efficiency and decrease in damage.

These studies and others of the Tavistock Institute have led Emery and Trist to conceptualize the enterprise as an 'open socio-technical system'. 'Open' because it is a system concerned with obtaining inputs from its environment and exporting outputs to its environment, as well as operating the conversion process in between. They regard the organization not in terms of a closed physical system which can obtain a stable resolution of forces in static equilibrium, but in the light of the modern biological concept of an open system (due to L. von Bertalanffy) in which the equilibrium obtained by the organism or the organization is essentially dynamic having a continual interchange across the boundaries with its environment. Indeed, they would regard the primary task of the management of the enterprise as a whole as that of relating the total system to its environment through the regulation of the boundary interchanges, rather than that of internal regulation. A management which takes its environment as given and concentrates on organizing internally in the most efficient way is pursuing a dangerous course. This does not mean that top management should not be involved in internal problems, but that such involvement must be oriented to the environmental opportunities and demands.

The problem is that environments are changing at an increasing rate and towards increasing complexity. Factors in the environment over which the organization has no control or even no knowledge, may interact to cause significant changes. Emery and Trist have classified environments according to their degree of complexity from that of a placid, randomized environment (corresponding to the economist's perfect competition) to that of a 'turbulent field' in which significant variances arise not only from competitive organizations involved but also from the field (e.g. market) itself. They present a case history of an organization which failed to appreciate that its environment was changing from a relatively placid to a relatively turbulent one. This company in the British food canning industry had, for a long period, held 65 per cent of the market for its main product – a tinned vegetable. On this basis the company invested in a new automatic factory, and in doing so incorporated an inbuilt rigidity – the necessity for long runs. But even whilst the factory was being built, several changes in the environment were taking place over which the organization had no control. The development of frozen foods, and the increasing affluence which enabled more people to afford these, presented consumers with an alternative. Greater direct competition came from the existence of surplus crops which American frozen food manufacturers sold off very cheaply due to their inappropriateness for freezing, their use by a number of small British *fruit* canning firms with surplus capacity due to the seasonal nature of imported fruit, and the development of supermarkets and chain stores with a wish to sell more goods under their house names. As the small canners provided an extremely cheap article (having no marketing costs and a cheaper raw material) they were able within three years to capture over 50 per cent of a shrinking market. This is a clear example of the way in which factors in the environment interact directly to produce a considerable turbulence in the field of the organization's operations, which, in the case of the vegetable canning factory, required a large redefinition of the firm's purpose, market and product mix before a new dynamic equilibrium was obtained.

The work of Trist and the Tavistock group has been most consistent in applying systems thinking over a large range of sites from the basic working group to the total enterprise, and in doing so has focussed on the dynamic nature of organizations and their functioning, the crucial importance of boundary management, and on the need for organizational effectiveness to be considered in its social and psychological, as well as its technological and economic aspects.

Bibliography

Organizational Choice, Tavistock, 1963.

TRIST, E. L., and BAMFORTH, K. W., 'Some social and psychological consequences of the longwall method of coal getting', *Hum. Rel.*, 1951, vol. 4, no. 1, pp. 3–38.

RICE, A. K., *Productivity and Social Organization*, Tavistock, 1958.

EMERY, F. E., and TRIST, E. L., 'Socio-technical systems', in Churchman, C. W., and Verhulst, M. (eds.), *Management Science, Models and Techniques*, vol. 2, Pergamon, 1960. Reprinted in Emery, F. E. (ed.), *Systems Thinking*, Penguin, 1969.

EMERY, F. E. and TRIST. E. L., 'The causal texture of organizational environments', *Hum. Rel.*, 1965, vol. 18, no. 1 pp. 21–32. Reprinted in F. E. Emery (ed.), *Systems Thinking*, Penguin, 1969.

2 The Functioning of Organizations

To manage is to forecast and plan, to organize, to command, to coordinate and to control.
Henri Fayol

A cooperative system is incessantly dynamic, a process of continual readjustment to physical, biological and social environments as a whole.
Chester I. Barnard

People move in the course of their daily work from a role in one system to a different role in another system; and it is essential that this be recognized and that behaviour appropriate to the role be adopted if trouble is to be avoided.
Wilfred Brown

If modification of the organization is involved, an understanding of the structure and dynamics of the thing acted upon is essential, so that the chain reaction of change in one part coursing through other parts can be calculated.
E. Wight Bakke

Organizational decisions depend on information, estimates and expectations that ordinarily differ appreciably from reality.
R. M. Cyert and J. G. March

Work expands so as to fill the time available for its completion.
C. Northcote Parkinson

In a hierarchy every employee tends to rise to his level of incompetence.
Laurence J. Peter

Accepting the likelihood of a number of types of organization, as writers on the structure of organizations suggest, is it feasible to think of analysing their activities? Is it possible to break down into categories what an organization does? Several theoretical schemes have been proposed for this purpose, applicable either to industrial enterprises or, more widely, to all organizations. Their originators have the view that some common classification is essential to bring order into the thoughts of those who try to understand organizations.

It is sometimes asserted that the functioning of each and every undertaking is unique. Taken literally, this gives us the prospect of a fund of interesting anecdotes about this or that enterprise, but no hope of lessons being drawn from the experience of one which will help another, or of a comprehensive theory which can be the basis for abstracting such lessons. However, most people do take it that there is some point in comparing their own organization with others, and learning from the comparison. Nor do administrators wilt in the face of the amorphous mass of activity going on in their undertakings without attempting some kind of analysis. Everyday managerial conversation abounds with categories such as service activities and direct production work, 'line' and 'staff', executive and administrative, and so on. Such concepts help to make sense of work situations which otherwise would defy analysis.

Attempts to develop unified analyses, offering widely applicable concepts, have been made by both managers and academics. Three top managers, one a Frenchman (Henri Fayol), one an American (Chester I. Barnard), and one an Englishman (Wilfred Brown), put forward analyses based on their personal insight and experience. E. Wight Bakke proposes a broad conceptualization derived from many years of sociologically based research into organizations, while R. M. Cyert and J. G. March attempt an analysis of organizational functioning derived from economic concepts.

In the sub-section on organizational practices,
C. Northcote Parkinson and Laurence J. Peter amusingly
but insightfully highlight certain practices of which
organizations must beware if they are to function
efficiently.

Henri Fayol

Henri Fayol (1841–1925) was a mining engineer by training. A Frenchman, he spent his working life with the French mining and metallurgical combine Commentry-Fourchamboult-Decazeville, first as an engineer but from his early thirties onwards in general management. From 1888 to 1918 he was Managing Director.

Fayol is among those who have achieved fame for ideas made known very late in life. He was in his seventies before he published them in a form which came to be widely read. He had written technical articles on mining engineering and a couple of preliminary papers on administration, but it was in 1916 that the *Bulletin de la Société de l'Industrie Minérale* printed Fayol's *Administration Industrielle et Générale – Prévoyance, Organization, Commandement, Coordination, Contrôle*. He is also among those whose reputation rests on a single short publication still frequently reprinted as a book; his other writings are little known.

The English version appears as *General and Industrial Management*, translated by Constance Storrs and first issued in 1949. There has been some debate over this rendering of the title of the work, and in particular of expressing the French word 'administration' by the term 'management'. It is argued that this could simply imply that Fayol is concerned only with industrial management, whereas his own preface claims that: 'Management plays a very important part in the government of undertakings; of all undertakings, large or small, industrial, commercial, political, religious or any other.' Indeed, in his last years he studied the problems of state public services and lectured at the École Supérieure de la Guerre. So it can be accepted that his intention was to initiate a theoretical analysis appropriate to a wide range of organizations.

Fayol suggests that: 'All activities to which industrial undertakings give rise can be divided into the following six groups:

1. Technical activities (production, manufacture, adaptation).
2. Commercial activities (buying, selling, exchange).
3. Financial activities (search for and optimum use of capital).
4. Security activities (protection of property and persons).
5. Accounting activities (stocktaking, balance sheet, costs, statistics).
6. Managerial activities (planning, organization, command, coordination, control).

Be the undertaking simple or complex, big or small, these six groups of activities or essential functions are always present.'

Most of these six groups of activities will be present in most jobs, but in varying measure, with the managerial element in particular being greatest in senior jobs and least or absent in direct production or lower clerical tasks. Managerial activities are specially emphasized as being universal to organizations. But it is a commonplace to ask: What is management? Is it anything that can be identified and stand on its own, or is it a word, a label, that has no substance?

Fayol's answer was unique at the time. The core of his contribution is his definition of management as comprising five elements:

1. To forecast and plan (in the French, *prévoyance*): 'examining the future and drawing up the plan of action'.
2. To organize: 'building up the structure, material and human, of the undertaking'.
3. To command: 'maintaining activity among the personnel'.
4. To coordinate: 'binding together, unifying and harmonizing all activity and effort'.
5. To control: 'seeing that everything occurs in conformity with established rule and expressed command'.

For Fayol, managing means looking ahead, which makes the

process of *forecasting and planning* a central business activity. Management must 'assess the future and make provision for it'. To function adequately a business organization needs a plan which has the characteristics of 'unity, continuity, flexibility and precision'. The problems of planning which management must overcome are: making sure that the objectives of each part of the organization are securely welded together (unity); using both short and long-term forecasting (continuity); being able to adapt the plan in the light of changing circumstances (flexibility); and attempting to accurately predict courses of action (precision). The essence of planning is to allow the optimum use of resources. Interestingly, Fayol in 1916 argued the necessity of a national plan for France, to be produced by the government.

To *organize* is 'building up the structure, material and human, of the undertaking'. The task of management is to build up an organization which will allow the basic activities to be carried out in an optimal manner. Central to this is a structure in which plans are efficiently prepared and carried out. There must be unity of command and direction, clear definition of responsibilities, precise decision-making backed up by an efficient system for selecting and training managers.

Fayol's third element comes logically after the first two. An organization must start with a plan, a definition of its goals. It then must produce an organization structure appropriate to the achievement of those goals. Third, the organization must be put in motion, which is *command*, maintaining activity among the personnel. Through his ability to command the manager obtains the best possible performance from his subordinates. This he does through example, knowledge of the business, knowledge of his subordinates, continuous contact with his staff, and by maintaining a broad view of his function. In this way he maintains a high level of activity by instilling a sense of mission.

Command refers to the relationship between a manager and the subordinates in his immediate task area. But organizations have a variety of tasks to perform, so *coordination* is necessary 'binding together, unifying and harmonizing all activity and effort'. Essentially this is making sure that one department's efforts are coincident with the efforts of other departments, and keeping all activities in perspective with regard to the overall aims of the organization. This can only be attained by a constant circulation of information and regular meetings of management.

Finally there is *control*, logically the final element which checks that the other four elements are in fact performing properly: 'seeing that everything occurs in conformity with established rule and expressed command.' To be effective, control must operate quickly and there must be a system of sanctions. The best way to ensure this is to separate all functions concerned with inspection from the operation departments whose work they inspect. Fayol believed in independent, impartial staff departments.

Fayol uses this classification to divide up his chapters on how to administer or manage. It is probable that when he wrote of '*une doctrine administrative*' he had in mind not only the above theory but the addition of experience to theoretical analysis to form a doctrine of good management. He summarizes the lessons of his own experience in a number of General Principles of Management. These are his own rules and he does not assume they are necessarily of universal application nor that they have any great permanence. Nonetheless, most have become part of managerial know-how and many are regarded as fundamental tenets. Fayol outlines the following fourteen principles:

1. Division of work: specialization allows the individual to build up expertise and thereby be more productive.

2. Authority: the right to issue commands, along with which must go the equivalent responsibility for its exercise.

3. Discipline: which is two-sided, for employees only obey orders if management play their part by providing good leadership.

4. Unity of command: in contrast to F. W. Taylor's functional authority (see p. 100), Fayol was quite clear that each man should have only one boss with no other conflicting lines

of command. On this issue history has favoured Fayol, for his principle has found most adherents among managers.

5. Unity of direction: people engaged in the same kind of activities must have the same objectives in a single plan.

6. Subordination of individual interest to general interest: management must see that the goals of the firm are always paramount.

7. Remuneration: payment is an important motivator, although by analysing a number of different possibilities, Fayol points out that there is no such thing as a perfect system.

8. Centralization or decentralization: again this is a matter of degree depending on the condition of the business and the quality of its personnel.

9. Scalar chain: a hierarchy is necessary for unity of direction but lateral communication is also fundamental as long as superiors know that such communication is taking place.

10. Order: both material order and social order are necessary. The former minimizes lost time and useless handling of materials. The latter is achieved through organization and selection.

11. Equity: in running a business, a 'combination of kindliness and justice' is needed in treating employees if equity is to be achieved.

12. Stability of tenure: this is essential due to the time and expense involved in training good management. Fayol believes that successful businesses tend to have more stable managerial personnel.

13. Initiative: allowing all personnel to show their initiative in some way is a source of strength for the organization even though it may well involve a sacrifice of 'personal vanity' on the part of many managers.

14. *Esprit de corps*: management must foster the morale of its employees and, to quote Fayol: 'real talent is needed to coordinate effort, encourage keenness, use each man's abilities,

and reward each one's merit without arousing possible jealousies and disturbing harmonious relations.'

But Fayol's pride of place in this field is due not so much to his principles of how to manage, enduring though these are, as to his definition of what management is. He is the earliest known proponent of a theoretical analysis of managerial activities – an analysis which has withstood almost a half-century of critical discussion. There can have been few writers since who have not been influenced by it; and his five elements have provided a system of concepts with which managers may clarify their thinking about what it is they have to do.

Bibliography

General and Industrial Management, Pitman, 1949. Translated by Constance Storrs from the original *Administration Industrielle et Générale*, 1916.

BRODIE, M. B., 'Henri Fayol: *Administration Industrielle et Générale*, a re-interpretation', *Public Admin.*, 1962, vol. 40, pp. 311–17.

BRODIE, M. B., *Fayol on Administration*, Lyon, Grant & Green, 1967.

Chester I. Barnard

Chester I. Barnard (1886–1961) was for many years President of the New Jersey Bell Telephone Company. On two occasions he was seconded for duty as State Director of the New Jersey Relief Administration, a government organization which allowed him many opportunities for contrasting the functioning of an established organization with one created *ad hoc* under conditions of stress. During the Second World War he developed and managed the United Service Organizations, Inc. As a practising top manager he had a continuing interest in describing organizational activities and the social and personal relationships between the people involved. This culminated in his classic book *The Functions of the Executive*, first published in 1938. His selected papers have also been published under the title *Organization and Management*.

Barnard begins his analysis from the premise that individuals must cooperate. This is because a human being has only limited power of choice, for he is confined partly by the situation in which he acts and partly by the biological restrictions of his nature. The most effective method of overcoming these limitations is cooperative social action. This requires that he adopt a group, or non-personal, purpose and take into consideration the processes of interaction. The persistence of cooperation depends on its effectiveness in accomplishing the cooperative purpose, and its efficiency in satisfying the individual's motives.

A formal organization for Barnard is a 'system of consciously coordinated activities or forces of two or more persons'. This definition, and the analysis based on it, can be applied to all forms of organization; the state, the church, the factory, the family. An organization comes into being when '(a) there are persons able to communicate with each other (b) who are willing to contribute action (c) to accomplish a common purpose'. Willingness to *contribute action* in this context means the surrender of the control of personal conduct in order to achieve coordination. Clearly the commitment of particular persons to do this will vary from maximum willingness through a neutral point to opposition or hatred. Indeed Barnard maintains that, in modern society, the majority of possible contributors to any given organization will lie on the negative side in their commitment. Equally important, the commitment of any individual will fluctuate, and thus the total willingness of all contributors to cooperate in any formal system is unstable – a fact which is evident from the history of all such organizations. Willingness to cooperate is the result of the satisfactions or dissatisfactions obtained, and all organizations depend upon the essentially subjective assessment of these made by the members.

All organizations have a *purpose*, but this does not produce cooperative activity unless it is accepted by the members. A purpose thus has both a cooperative and a subjective aspect. The subjective aspect is not the meaning of the purpose to the individual but rather what the individual thinks it means to the organization as a whole. Thus a man will carry out a job he dislikes if he accepts it as relevant to the aim of the whole organization and to his part in it. The essential basis for cooperative action is a cooperative purpose which is *believed* by the contributors to be that of the organization. 'The inculcation of belief in the real existence of a common purpose is an essential executive function.' The continuance of an organization depends on its ability to carry out its purpose, but there is the paradox that it destroys itself by accomplishing its objectives, as is shown by the large number of successful organizations which disappear through failure to renew them. Continuing organizations require the repeated adoption of new purposes. This process is often concealed by stating a generalized purpose which appears not to change, e.g. giving a service, making motor-cars. But the real purpose is not 'service' as an abstraction, but specific acts of service; not making motor-cars in general, but making specific motor-cars from day to day.

The other essential for a formal organization is *communication*, linking the common purpose with those willing to cooperate in it. Communication is necessary to translate purpose into action. The methods of communication are firstly language – oral and written – and, secondly, 'observational feeling'. This is the ability to understand, without words, not merely the situation but also the intention. It results from special experience and training and continuity in association, which leads the members of the organization to develop common perceptions and reactions to particular situations.

Large organizations are made up of numbers of basic units. These units are small – from two to fifteen persons – and are limited in their growth by the limitations of intercommunication. The size of a unit depends on the complexity of the purpose and the technological conditions for action, the difficulty of the communication process, the extent to which communication is necessary, and the complexity of the personal relationships involved. These last increase with great rapidity as the number of persons in the unit group increases. Moreover, groups are related to each other. As the number of possible groups increases, the complexity of group relationships increases in greater ratio.

Interactions between persons which are based on personal rather than joint or common purposes will, because of their repetitive character, become systematic and organized. This will be the informal organization, which will have an important effect on the thought and action of the members. Barnard envisages a continual interaction between formal and informal organization. An informal organization to be effective – particularly if it is of any size – must give rise to formal organization, which makes explicit many of its attitudes and institutions. Formal organizations once established must create, if they are to operate effectively, informal organizations as a means of communication and cohesion and as a way of protecting the integrity of the individual against domination by the formal organization. This last function may seem to operate against the aims of the formal organization, but it is in fact vital to it. For it is by giving the individual a sphere where he is able to exercise personal choice and not have his decisions dominated by the impersonal objectives of the formal organization, that the personality of the individual is safeguarded and his continuing effective contribution to the formal organization made more likely.

On the basis of his analysis of organizational functioning, Barnard describes the functions of the executive. The members of the executive organization are contributors to two units in a complex organization – a basic working unit and an executive unit. Thus a foreman is regarded as a member of a shop group as well as of the department management group; an army captain is a member of his company and of the 'regimental organization'. Under such conditions a single action is an activity of two different unit organizations. It is this simultaneous contribution which makes the complex organization into an organic whole.

It is important to recognize that not all work carried out by the executive is executive work. Executive work is 'the specialized work of *maintaining* the organization in operation' and consists of three tasks:

1. The maintenance of organizational communication.
2. The securing of essential services from individuals.
3. The formulation of purpose and objectives.

The task of *communication* has two phases: the first is the definition of organizational positions – the 'scheme of organization'. This requires organization charts, specification of duties, and the like. It represents a coordination of the work to be done. But the scheme of organization is of little value without the personnel to fill the positions. The second phase of the task of communication is the recruiting of contributors who have the appropriate qualifications. But both phases are dependent on each other. 'Men are neither good nor bad but only good or bad in this or that position'; and often the scheme of organization has to be changed to take account of the men available. The informal executive organization has the function of expanding the means of communication and thus reducing the need for formal decisions. The issuing of formal decisions, except for routine matters and for emergencies, is unnecessary with a good informal organization. In this situation, a formal order is the recognition that agreement has been obtained on the decision by informal means. It is part of the art of leadership to eschew conflict in formal order-giving by issuing only those formal orders which are acceptable. Disagreements must be dealt with by informal means.

The task of *securing the essential services* from individuals has two main divisions: bringing persons into cooperative relationship with the organization, and eliciting the services of such people. Both are achieved by maintaining morale, and by maintaining schemes of incentives, deterrents, supervision and control, and education and training.

The third executive task is the *formulation of the purposes* of the organization. The critical aspect here is 'the assignment of responsibility – the delegation of objective authority'. Responsibility for abstract long-term decisions on purpose lies with the executive organization, but responsibility for action remains at the base. The definition of purpose in particular situations is a widely distributed function; hence there is a need to indoctrinate those at the lower levels with general purposes and major decisions, if the organization is to be a cohesive organic whole.

As a practising manager in industry and in public service Barnard has combined a thorough knowledge of the workings of organization with a wide reading of sociology. As a result his work has had a great impact on the thinking both of managers and of academics.

Bibliography

The Functions of the Executive, Harvard University Press, 1938.
Organization and Management, Harvard University Press, 1948.

Wilfred Brown

For over twenty years Wilfred Brown was Chairman of the Glacier Metal Company, and was also Managing Director for most of that period. Glacier Metal, which manufactures bearings, is the company which since 1949 has been the subject of the very well-known studies begun by the Tavistock Institute of Human Relations and continued by Elliott Jaques (see p. 131) in a consultant capacity. Wilfred Brown, therefore, has both long experience as a practising manager and a long-standing acquaintance with social research. His ideas are derived from his own experience and he does not claim that they are necessarily appropriate outside the engineering industry. Nonetheless, he argues that: 'The absence of a language, concepts and a general theory of administration is a serious impediment to the efficiency of industry.' He himself aims at clarifying what he believes happens in organizations.

Brown breaks away from the kind of analysis initiated by Fayol which describes management as a mixture of elements such as forecasting, planning, organizing. Brown is less concerned with the nature of a manager's activities as such than with the social organization, or set of social systems, through which the manager works. His fundamental tenet is that a conscious recognition of these social systems will promote good management.

Brown proceeds to distinguish three social systems whose structures taken together are the organization of a company:

1. The Executive System
2. The Representative System
3. The Legislative System

The *executive system* is the structure of roles more commonly referred to as the organization chart or hierarchy (including operators, clerks, etc., as well as managers or executives). It exists irrespective of people. Individuals may come and go but the role does not disappear. New roles can be added to the system before any thought is given to who should fill them. The work content of roles can increase or decrease in importance without the persons in the roles changing their personal capacity to do the work. Because this social structure exists as an entity in itself it can be consciously thought about and altered.

Brown contends that 'there seems to be quite a considerable tendency to construe all problems in industry in terms of the personal behaviour of people, and to exclude the notion that we can design trouble into, or out of, an executive system.' Thus people blame difficulties on to the personalities of others, or blame their own personality, seldom stopping to think whether the difficulty results from the design of the social system of which their own roles are a part.

Brown suggests that wherever there is an executive system there will be within it, or alongside it, a *representative system* to convey the views and feelings of subordinates to superiors. There may be no explicit recognition of this role structure, but it exists nonetheless. For example, a managing director who introduces changes will be faced with *ad hoc* deputations; groups with grievances to air will send forward spokesmen. Individuals in these representative roles are not necessarily stating their own views, of course, and cannot be held responsible by their managers as would be the case if they were acting in their executive roles. In Glacier Metal, representatives are formally elected by all levels of employees.

Brown's concept of the *legislative system* differs from his concepts of executive and representative systems. Each of the latter is a separate series of interrelated roles occupied by people, but the legislative system is the interaction of four related role systems. These are the shareholders and directors, the customers, the representative system and the executive system. Each of these four role systems has very considerable power *vis-à-vis* a company. Their power circumscribes what the company may do and their interaction legislates, in effect, for what is done.

Thus when a chief executive feels that action is required which exceeds his authority he may refer to the board, or a shareholders' meeting, or test customers' reaction through a sales organization. In effect, these then interact with the executive and representative systems. Glacier Metal have established councils for the purpose of legislating on general principles; for example, stating the obligations of employees on hours of work. Councils are composed of representatives and management members, but do not have executive authority. Through them the representative and executive systems are brought into contact, and discussions are conducted with the reactions of board, shareholders, and customers in mind.

In the course of his discussion of the executive system, Brown makes an analysis of the *Operational Work and Specialist Work* of businesses which is in contrast to, say, Bakke's analysis of activities. In Brown's view, all businesses carry out three functions, namely development, production and sales, which at Glacier Metal are called 'operational work'. But he also holds that 'all work activity implies a manning of activity, a technique of activity and a chosen quantified and timed deployment of activity on a particular operational task'. Hence each of the three categories of operational activity – development, management and sales – may be thought of as having three possible dimensions of specialist work, a personnel aspect (organizational and personnel), a technical aspect (concerned with production techniques), and a programming aspect (balancing, timing and quantification of operations). Specialists arise in all these aspects. There may be personnel officers, engineers, production controllers, chemists, and many more. Glacier have organized these specialists in divisions corresponding to Brown's analysis, a Personnel Division, a Technical Division, and a Programming Division, whose specialist work supports the three operational work functions. Specialists are attached to the various levels of operational (or line) managers.

In *Piecework Abandoned* Brown is concerned with methods of payment rather than with organization, but his conclusions stem from the same mode of thinking to be found in *Exploration in Management*. Under payment by results manager–worker relationships are different from the relationships under time rates; that is, the actual organization is different. He takes the view that the 'full managerial role' should include knowing subordinates, assessing their performance and being responsible for it, and deciding whether or not they are acceptable for the roles required. Then a full manager–subordinate relationship exists in which subordinates are assessed on their whole behaviour and they are aware of their accountability to their manager. Wage incentive systems lay across this relationship a bargaining relationship in which the worker becomes a sub-contractor and the foreman abdicates the full managerial role. Thus the organization is changed. Employees are not held to account for loss of output because as sub-contractors they are 'paying' for it themselves. They cease to hold full responsible roles in the organization and regard lost time as their own affair. Using the same argument, Brown also attacks time-clocks which have the same effects on the role structure and behaviour as does piecework. Both wage incentives and clocking-on have been abandoned at Glacier's factories.

Brown's originality as a writer on management is in his use of the concepts of 'structure' and 'role'. His insistence on detached analysis using these concepts leads him to conclude that: 'Effective organization is a function of the work to be done and the resources and techniques available to do it.'

Bibliography

Exploration in Management, Heinemann, 1960.
Piecework Abandoned, Heinemann, 1962.

BROWN, W., and JAQUES, E., *Glacier Project Papers*, Heinemann, 1965.

E. Wight Bakke

E. Wight Bakke has been at the Labor and Management Center of Yale University for many years, and his work is associated with that of Argyris (see p. 135) of the Department of Industrial Administration at the same University. Bakke has concerned himself with the general problem of the integration of people into organizations, but before his work developed in this direction he was interested in unemployment. In 1931 he investigated the plight of the unemployed worker in Britain.

Bakke's work on organization theory is focused on the problem of developing concepts and meaningful words to denote them, with which to define and analyse organizations and their activities. Some order must be brought into the miscellany of findings from research and from the lessons of experience. His aim is to create theoretical means of analysis which can be applied not only to economic organizations but to schools, churches and so forth. This confronts him with the task of reducing the seemingly endless diversity of forms of human social organization to some kind of common elements.

Bakke begins by thinking of a social organization as a continuing system of differentiated and coordinated human activities which welds together resources into a whole that has a character all its own. Of itself, this definition is perhaps no more than a truism, but by thinking in these terms Bakke makes the task of analysis a little clearer. If indeed it is useful to conceptualize a social organization as a system of activities, then a classification of activities is needed. If in addition it is useful to see those activities as operating on resources, then a classification of resources is a necessary complement.

The basic *resources* essential to the operation of an organization are held to fall under one of six headings. These are human, material (raw materials, and equipment), financial, natural (natural resources not processed by human activity) and ideational (the ideas used by the organization and the language in which these are communicated). There is also the organization's operational field, e.g. for a company its sales market, or for a trade union the labour market. Bakke's intention is that these categories, not unfamiliar for the most part, should be so defined as to be appropriate to the resources employed by any kind of 'specific purpose' social organization; be it economic, military, religious, or any other. Similarly, he contends that all the *activities* of such organizations can be fitted into one or other of five categories: perpetuation, workflow, control, identification and homeostasis.

It is axiomatic that if an organization is to continue in being, resources of the kinds listed above must be available to it. Activities which ensure this availability are called *perpetuation activities*. In industry, for example, the buying department discovers sources of supply of raw materials and endeavours to sustain the required supply. Perpetuation of personnel is achieved by appointing new people and instructing them in their duties, an activity which may be specialized in a personnel department. A meeting to consider a share issue may be classified as a finance-perpetuating activity.

Workflow activities comprise all that is done to create and distribute the output of an organization, whether that output is a product or a service. A wide range of activities can be classified in this way. For example, a production activity in an organization might be a telephone exchange operator making connections for trunk calls, or an assembly worker sealing tops on car batteries, or an army crew driving a tank on manoeuvres. On the distribution side are sales activities, etc.

Bakke groups under *control activities* all activities designed to coordinate and unify. He breaks these down into four subcategories:

1. Directive activities, being those which initiate action, such as determining what shall be done and to what standard, and giving instruction. For example, a foreman allocating jobs.

2. Motivation activities, rewarding or penalizing behaviour, e.g. an office supervisor recommending a salary increase for a clerk, or a foreman recommending discharge of a worker.

3. Evaluation activities, e.g. reviewing and appraising people's performance, comparing alternative courses of action.

4. Communication activities, providing people with the premises and data they need.

If the character of an organization, or charter as it may be called, is to be reflected in a commonly held image of the organization in the minds of its members and of outsiders, activities must be carried out which define this charter and symbolize it. These are *identification activities*. Instances are an article in the company magazine stressing the unique qualities of the service the company has always given, or an address by the chairman on the history and traditions of the undertaking.

Bakke argues that the four types of activity so far outlined must be so arranged and regulated that they maintain the organization in existence, in a state enabling it competently to perform its function. In short, there must be what he calls *homeostatic activities*, which preserve the organization in 'dynamic equilibrium'. These activities are of four kinds: the fusion process, the problem-solving process, the leadership process and the legitimization process.

The concept fundamental to Bakke's 'fusion process' theory is that both individuals and organizations are entities striving for 'self-realization'. In this he and Argyris (see p. 135) think on much the same lines. An organization attempts to shape in its own image all the individuals who join it, and an individual who joins an organization likewise tries to express his own personality by shaping the organization accordingly. Each experiences some change, but there may be times when the organization and its members are mutually opposed. Hence the need for fusion process activities to reconcile, harmonize or 'fuse' organization, groups and individuals. (W. H. Whyte pillories some of these activities – see p. 164.) In the same way, an organization has to be more or less integrated with a diversity of other organizations outside itself, and the process of accommodating divergent interests can again be thought of as fusion. Bakke himself has given particular attention to this idea of fusion processes, looking on it as a single frame of reference with which to simplify thinking about the array of human problems in organizations which are encountered in research and in daily experience.

The continual solving of non-routine problems in an organization is termed the problem-solving process, and Bakke sets out, in his contribution to the symposium edited by Mason Haire (1959), what he believes to be a logical sequence of steps normally taken in problem-solving. Bakke also distinguishes a leadership process, providing imagination and initiative. Finally, there is the legitimization process – activities to justify and get accepted the ends of the organization and what it does to pursue them. Thus a company secretary registering articles of association is performing a legitimization activity, for these articles state what the company has a legal right to do. Similarly, managers frequently persuade other people (and each other) that the organization's products are beneficial to those who use them, and that the organization is a good thing for all involved in it and for society. Ultimately, an organization cannot survive without acceptance of its legitimacy.

The idea of *homeostatic activities* is intended to apply to a very wide variety of organizations, but taking work organizations in particular it appears to have much in common with what is usually meant by the words management or administration.

The point of constructing a theoretical framework, in the way Bakke does, is to clarify thinking. Does it help to make sense of what before seemed too complicated? Does it make like and unlike comparable, when before they seemed to defy comparison? Bakke is less concerned with management

as such than Fayol or Barnard or Brown, and the test of his
contribution is whether, after any initial feelings of strangeness
have been overcome, managers and researchers find that the
use of his concepts helps them in their understanding.

Bibliography

The Unemployed Worker, Yale University Press, 1933.

Bonds of Organization, Harper & Row, 1950.

The Fusion Process: An Interim Report, Labor and Management
Center, Yale University, 1953.

'Concept of the social organization', in Mason Haire (ed.),
Modern Organization Theory, pp. 16–75, Chapman & Hall,
1959. Also published by the Labor and Management Center,
Yale University (revised edn).

Richard M. Cyert and James G. March

Richard Cyert and James March between them epitomize the development of the school of decision-making theory at what is now Carnegie-Mellon University. March's interest in processes of decision is also reflected in the distinctive sophistication of his many publications on the nature of power. Cyert is Dean of the Graduate School of Industrial Administration at Carnegie-Mellon University, Pittsburgh, and March is Professor of Psychology and Sociology at the University of California, Irvine.

Their 'behavioural theory of the firm' is a notable effort to link classical economics theory to contemporary organization theory. It is an attempt to describe and to explain how business decisions come to be made. Cyert and March take business firms as their starting point, and specifically have in mind the large multi-product organization operating under 'imperfect competition', that is, in a market where supply of and demand for the product do not move freely but can be manipulated by the firms in limited competition. The theory is about decisions such as what price to aim at, what volume to produce, and how resources are to be allocated within a firm. Decisions of these kinds are seen as choices, made in terms of objectives, from among a set of alternatives on the basis of whatever information is available.

Classical theory tends to view a firm as an entrepreneur rather than as an organization, and, assuming perfect knowledge of all market conditions, stresses profit maximization as the goal. It takes a firm to be an 'omnisciently rational' system of business.

Cyert and March view a firm as an 'adaptively rational'

system, adapting and responding to a variety of internal and external constraints in arriving at decisions.

Far from showing the characteristics of a single-minded entrepreneur, a business organization is composed of a number of departments with diverse interests. Decisions have to allow for these interests. But what guide-lines or rules then set limits to decisions? Far from having perfect knowledge, organizations appear to act on very small portions of the total available information. If this is so, then the means by which these small selections of information come to be screened out are critical. How are they affected by internal conflicts or by pressure of time? So a business firm is constrained by its problems of internal management coordination, by the uncertainty of its external situation or environment, and by its own limited capacity for assembling, storing and utilizing information.

What does a firm look like as an information-processing and decision-making system? To begin with, it is not tidily monolithic. It is more like a shifting multiple-goal coalition. In a business organization the coalition includes managers, workers, stockholders, suppliers, customers, lawyers, tax collectors, regulatory agencies, etc., all of whom have some interest in the organization but whose goals or preferences about what should be done potentially differ. More than this, the organization splits the decisions in which coalition members are interested into sub-problems and assigns the sub-problems to sub-units in the organization. In a departmental structure, the sales department handles marketing problems, the accounting department handles finance problems, and so on. Each such sub-unit sees its own objectives as paramount for the goals of the firm as a whole.

Thus just as a manager needs to predict and attempt to manipulate the unstable external environment of his firm, he must predict and attempt to manipulate its internal complexities. Cyert and March have the impression that most managers devote much more time and energy to the problems of managing the 'coalition' than they do to the problems of dealing with the outside world. Decisions cannot be taken without an intricate reckoning of the interests involved and the demands of all who are interested. One result is a 'fire department' organization in which decisions are actually taken as things happen on the basis of immediate expediency, and not on the basis of far-sighted cool calculation as is supposed. For example, sales may be forecast and long-term production plans carefully developed, but actual production decisions are more often affected by the day to day impact of salesmen's reports, recent sales figures and inventory levels. Yet this is not so irrational as it may seem. Given that a firm is indeed a multiple-goal coalition of interests, then the firm may have learned that this pattern of behaviour best permits continual adjustment to the shifting demands of those interests.

The decision process concerns three basic characteristics of organizations, organizational goals, organizational expectations and organizational choice. That is, what shall the objectives be, what is expected to happen and what consequences are anticipated from actions which could be taken, and what action shall be chosen.

There are four features of the decision-making process, which as relational concepts taken together form a theory to explain how these decisions are arrived at. They are:

1. Quasi-resolution of conflict
2. Uncertainty avoidance
3. Problemistic search
4. Organizational learning.

Quasi-resolution of conflict describes the internal condition of most organizations most of the time. Even if there is consensus of vague overall goals, when it comes to the statement of objectives to be acted upon there is no consensus. An organization is a coalition of conflicting interests. Nor do the devices for 'quasi-resolution' of these conflicts actually arrive at consensus; what they do is to enable organizations to thrive despite unresolved divergencies. The first such device is 'local rationality'. As each sub-unit or department deals with only one set of decision problems it solves these 'rationally' within its own narrow specialist perspective whether or not the total outcome for the organization over the range of sub-units is rational. Sales departments handle sales decisions and production departments production ones, and so a complex set of interrelated problems is reduced to separate simple ones even though the decisions then taken on each may be mutually inconsistent.

The second device for quasi-resolution of conflict eases this difficulty. It is 'acceptable level decision rules'. Overall optimization by the firm might require each decision to be consistent with all the others; but in fact the acceptable level of consistency is low enough to permit an outcome which is simply acceptable to all interests, rather than optimal to anything overall. Thirdly, 'sequential attention to goals' also helps to quasi-resolve conflict. Rather than commit itself to one goal or another, an organization attends first to one goal and then to another in sequence, e.g. it resolves pressures for 'smooth production' versus 'satisfy customers' (with individual design modifications) by doing first one and then the other.

Uncertainty is something with which all organizations must live. There are market uncertainties, uncertainties over supplies, uncertainties over the behaviour of shareholders and governments, and so on. But the decision processes in organizations act to avoid uncertainty. They avoid having to act on long-term forecasts by actually reacting to information here and now, and solve pressing problems rather than develop long-run strategies. They avoid having to anticipate external events by arranging a 'negotiated environment'. That is, long contracts with suppliers and customers, adherence to industry-wide pricing conventions, and support of stable 'good business practice'.

Classical theories of choice in economics focussed on the problem of choice among limited alternatives, but ignored the importance of the process of search by which the alternatives were found. *Problemistic search* is the means used by organizations to determine what choices are thought to be available. Regular planned search such as routine accumulation of market information is relatively unimportant. Search is 'motivated', i.e. the occurrence of a problem spurs search for ways to handle or solve it, and once a way is found (which includes revising objectives to fit available action) then search stops. So pet projects (e.g. costs to be cut in someone else's department) look for crises to fit them (e.g. a fall in profits).

Secondly, search is 'simple-minded'. When a problem arises, search for a new solution is concentrated near the old solution. A problem is assumed to concern a particular department within whose field it apparently falls, and this department then examines possibilities not too different from whatever it is that has failed, using the limited information available to it from previously established recording and filing procedures and using personnel trained in existing standard 'good practice'. If no answer appears, search turns to vulnerable areas (e.g. research) that cannot easily demonstrate their necessity by concrete results. Thirdly, therefore, search bias inhibits radically new alternatives.

Finally, *organizational learning* takes place in the decision-making process. That is, adaptation occurs through the individual members of the organization. Adaptation of goals is brought about by assessing relevant past experience of the organization and of other comparable organizations. Changing goals bring adaptation in attention, different sets of events or problems being considered. In particular, sub-units pay most attention to those criteria of good performance on which they are usually shown to be performing well. Similarly, continual failure to find acceptable solutions eventually brings adaptation of search rules.

In summary, organizational goals change in response to the sub-goals or interests of those who form the coalition, to a minimal level of what will be accepted all round, after restricted examination of a limited and selective range of information. In this way, the full complexity of decision-making is reduced to what is practicable, and uncertainty is absorbed. Organizational expectations of what may happen are likewise confined to a number of possibilities few enough and familiar enough to be practicable; and organizational choices are made from among the resulting limited alternatives. For example, budget allocations to projects or to sub-units are the outcome of a bargaining-type interaction between the interests of coalition members, rather than of abstract problem-solving calculation. The main difference between project allocation and sub-unit allocation is that sub-units last longer than projects, so historical precedents are of greater importance.

The behavioural theory of the firm at first appears to make no sense on the question of innovation. In principle it should be possible to predict who will introduce what kind of innovation, and when. Products change, customer preferences change: what innovations will there be? The theory has argued that search is motivated by the occurrence of a problem. Failure to find a solution induces further search. Consequently, it would be predicted that, everything else being equal, relatively unsuccessful firms would be more likely to innovate than relatively successful firms. But what evidence there is just does not support this. There is a further complication in the notion of 'organizational slack'. Slack is the difference between the payments required to maintain the organization and the resources obtained from the environment by the coalition. In general, success breeds slack, i.e. resources surplus to the costs of maintaining the organization. Such slack is channelled to suit the particular aims of particular sub-units and individuals, giving scope for economies if these are necessary later. So it provides funds for innovations desired by sub-units of a kind which would not be approved in times of scarcity. If so, then the theory now predicts innovation in both unsuccessful *and* successful firms.

The solution to this puzzle may come from distinguishing two kinds of innovation – problem-oriented innovation and slack innovation. Problem-oriented innovation results from a search for justifiable short-run solutions directly linked to the problems of unsuccessful firms; slack innovation is difficult to justify in the short-run and results from sub-unit and individual exploitation of resources in successful firms.

Although the book in which Cyert and March draw their

Organizational Practices

C. Northcote Parkinson

Cyril Northcote Parkinson, an English political scientist, graduated from Emmanuel College, Cambridge. One-time Professor of History at the University of Malaya and Visiting Professor at Harvard and Illinois, he has written many works on historical, political and economic subjects.

Parkinson confronts the manifest fact that there is little or no relationship between the work to be done in an organization and the size of staff doing it. The growth of administrative hierarchies may be independent of the work itself. To explain this phenomenon he propounds Parkinson's Law that 'work expands to fill the time available for its completion'.

As a graphic analogy with the world of administration, he cites the case of the elderly lady with nothing else to do, who spends an entire day sending a postcard to her niece, ending 'prostrate after a day of doubt, anxiety, and toil'.

Small wonder, then, that administrative officials find themselves overworked. What they will do about it is foretold by the motivational axiom 'an official wants to multiply subordinates, not rivals'. Hence rather than share the work with colleague B, overworked official A appoints subordinates C and D. By appointing two, A preserves his own position of being the only official comprehending the entire range of work. When C inevitably complains of overwork, A preserves equity by allowing C to have subordinates E and F and also by allowing D to appoint G and H. With this staff, A's own promotion is now virtually certain. Moreover, by this stage a second axiom has taken effect, 'officials make work for each other'. For seven are now doing what one did before, but the routing of drafts, minutes and incoming documents between them ensures that all are working hard and that A is working harder than ever.

Parkinson cites impressive evidence of this process. The British Navy Estimates disclose that over the first half of this century whilst the numbers of ships and of officers and men declined, the numbers of Admiralty and dockyard officials increased rapidly. Indeed, the men of Whitehall increased nearly 80 per cent, and it may be concluded that this would have occurred had there been no seamen at all. Similarly in the Colonial Office. In 1947 and again in 1954 the figures for staff had risen substantially even though during and after the war the size of the Empire had markedly shrunk.

Once constituted, administrative hierarchies are bestrewn with committees, councils and boards, through which the weightier matters of finance must pass. Now since a million is real only to a millionaire, these committees and the like are necessarily made up of persons accustomed to think in tens or hundreds, perhaps in thousands, but never more than this. The result is a typical pattern of committee work which may be stated as the Law of Triviality. It means 'that the time spent on any item of the agenda will be in inverse proportion to the sum involved'.

Thus a contract for a £10,000,000 atomic reactor will be passed with a murmur of agreement, after formal reference to the engineers' and the geophysicists' reports and to plans in appendices. In such cases the Law of Triviality is supplemented by technical factors, since half the committee including the chairman do not know what a reactor is and half the rest do not know what it is for. Rather than face these difficulties of explanation, any member who does know will decide it is better to say nothing despite his misgivings about the whole thing. However, when the agenda reaches the question of a roof for the bicycle shed for the clerical staff, here is both a topic and a sum of money which everyone understands. Now all can show they are pulling their weight and make up for their silence over the reactor. Discussion will go on for at least forty-five minutes, and a saving of some £100 may be satisfactorily achieved.

Of course, such a committee will have passed the size of approximately 21 members, which Parkinson's Coefficient of Inefficiency (he proposes a formula for this) predicts as critical. Where such a number is reached, conversations occur at both ends of the table, and to be heard a member has to rise. Once on his feet, he cannot help making a speech, if only from force of habit. At this point the efficient working of a committee becomes impossible.

This might have happened in any case from self-induced 'injelitis' – the disease of induced inferiority. From an examination of moribund institutions it has been ascertained that the source infection comes from the arrival in an organization's hierarchy of an individual combining both incompetence (as forecast by Peter, see p. 91) and jealousy. At a certain concentration these qualities react to induce 'injelitance', soon the head of the organization, who is second-rate, sees to it that his subordinates are all third-rate, and they see to it that their subordinates are fourth-rate, and so on. The organization accepts its mediocrity and ceases to attempt to match better organizations. After all, since little is done mistakes are rare, and since aims are low, success is complete.

The characteristics of organizations can be assessed even more easily than this, simply by their physical accoutrements. Publishers, for example, or again research establishments, frequently flourish in shabby and makeshift quarters. Lively and productive as these may be, who is not impressed by the contrasting institution with an imposing and symmetrical façade, within which shining floors glide to a receptionist murmuring with carmine lips into an ice-blue receiver.

However, it is now known that a perfection of planned layout is achieved only by institutions on the point of collapse. During exciting discovery or progress there is no time to plan the perfect headquarters. This comes afterwards – and too late. Thus by the time the Palace of Nations at Geneva was opened in 1937 the League had practically ceased to exist. The British Empire expanded whilst the Colonial Office was in haphazard accommodation, and contracted after it moved into purpose-built accommodation in 1875. The conduct of the Second World War was planned in crowded and untidy premises in Washington, the elaborate layout of the Pentagon at Arlington, Virginia, being constructed later.

In public affairs there is a propensity for expenditure on elaborate and inappropriate constructions such as those mentioned, as indeed for any other kind of expenditure. In fact, all forms of administration are prone to expenditure. This is due to the effects of Parkinson's Second Law that 'expenditure rises to meet income'. The widely understood domestic phenomenon which unfailingly appears after each increase in the husband's income is equally prevalent in administration. With the important difference in government administration, that expenditure rises toward a ceiling that is not there. Were revenue to be reduced there would actually be an improvement in services. The paradox of administration is that if there were fewer officials each would have *less* to do and therefore more time to think about what he was doing.

Bibliography

Parkinson's Law, and Other Studies in Administration, Murray, 1958; Penguin, 1965.
The Law and the Profits, Murray, 1960; Penguin, 1965.

Laurence J. Peter

Laurence J. Peter was born in Canada, and studied education at Washington State University. Currently Associate Professor of Education at the University of Southern California, his work concerns emotionally disturbed and retarded children. He has been a school psychologist, prison instructor, counsellor, and consultant. Raymond Hull, born in England, has lived in British Columbia since 1947. He has written many plays for television and stage production and articles for leading periodicals. He also wrote Peter's principle into a book; Peter himself having reached a level in the University hierarchy where he was unable to do anything about it!

This latter fact can be understood by hierarchiologists (those who study hierarchies), from The Peter Principle. Derived from the analysis of the hundreds of cases of incompetence in organizations which can be seen anywhere, the Principle states that 'in a hierarchy every employee tends to rise to his level of incompetence', and it applies to all organizations.

The Principle assumes a constant quest for high performance. Hence people competent at their jobs are promoted so that they may do still better. Competence in each new position qualifies for promotion to the next, until each individual arrives at a job beyond his abilities and therefore no longer performs in a way that gains further promotion. This is his level of incompetence. Given two conditions, enough ranks in the hierarchy to provide promotions and enough time to move through them, all employees rise to and remain at their level of incompetence. This can be stated as Peter's Corollary: 'In time, every post tends to be occupied by an employee who is incompetent to carry out its duties.' Every employee ultimately achieves Peter's Plateau at which his Promotion Quotient (PQ) is zero.

How then is any work ever accomplished? Work is done by those who have not yet reached their level of incompetence. There can be occasional instances of 'summit competence' where competent company chairmen or victorious field marshals have not yet had time to reach their level of incompetence. Frequently such persons side-step into another field whose hierarchy enables them to attain a level of incompetence not available to them before. In general, classical pyramidal structures divided horizontally by a class barrier are more efficient than classless or equalitarian hierarchies. Beneath the class barrier many employees remain, unable to rise high enough to reach their level of incompetence. They spend their whole careers on tasks they can do well. Above the class barrier the pyramid apex narrows rapidly, thus holding below their incompetence level many who joined because of opportunities of starting at this high point in the hierarchy. Aptitude tests for promotion candidates do not in fact foster efficiency, the main difference being that tested people reach their levels of incompetence sooner.

There are two main methods of accelerating promotion to the incompetence level, namely Pull and Push. Pull is defined as 'an employee's relationship – by blood, marriage, or acquaintance – with a person above him in the hierarchy'. Push is usually shown by an abnormal interest in training and general self-improvement. The question is which of these two methods is most effective? The force of Push is overestimated, for it is normally overcome by the downward pressure of the Seniority Factor. Pull, of course is comparatively unaffected by this, which yields the dictum 'never Push when you can Pull'.

Non-hierarchiologists are sometimes deceived by apparent exceptions to the Peter Principle. Being 'kicked upstairs' or sideways to a job with a longer title in a remote building are mistakenly thought to contravene the Principle. But the Principle applies only to genuine promotions *from* a level of competence, whereas both the above cases are pseudo-promotions between levels of incompetence.

Another error is in the notion of what is success. It is said that 'nothing succeeds like success'. In fact, hierarchiology shows that nothing fails like success. What is called 'success' the hierarchiologist recognizes as *final placement*. The so-called success ailments such as ulcers, colitis, insomnia, dermatitis and sexual impotence constitute the Final Placement Syndrome typical of those working beyond their level of competence.

Obviously, the longer a hierarchy has been established the less useful work will be done, and eventually no useful work may be done at all (as in the injelitis coma discussed by Parkinson, see p. 89). Parkinson's theory holds that as work expands to fill available time so more subordinate officials are appointed, whose arrival necessarily expands the work further, and so on. Hence hierarchical expansion. But the Peter Principle shows that the expansion is due to a genuine striving for efficiency. Those who have reached their levels of incompetence seek desperately some means of overcoming their inadequacy, and as a last resort appoint more staff to see if this will help. This is the reason why there is no direct relationship between the size of the staff and the amount of useful work done.

Bibliography

PETER, L. J., and HULL, R., *The Peter Principle*, William Morrow, 1969.

3 The Management of Organizations

Scientific management will mean, for the employers and the workmen who adopt it, the elimination of almost all causes for dispute and disagreement between them.
Frederick W. Taylor

How can we avoid the two extremes; too great bossism in giving orders, and practically no orders given? ... My solution is to depersonalize the giving of orders, to unite all concerned in a study of the situation, to discover the law of the situation and obey that.
Mary Parker Follett

I am convinced that a logical scheme of organization, a structure based on principles, which take priority over personalities, is in the long run far better both for the morale of an undertaking as a whole and for the happiness of individuals, than the attempt to build one's organization round persons.
Lyndall F. Urwick

The task of administration is so to design the environment that the individual will approach as close as practicable to rationality (judged in terms of the organization's goals) in his decisions.
Herbert A. Simon

The needs of large-scale organization have to be satisfied by common people achieving uncommon performance.
Peter F. Drucker

An organization does not make decisions; its function is to provide a framework, based on established criteria, within which decisions can be fashioned in an orderly manner.
Alfred P. Sloan Jr

Organizations with differing structures, functioning in different ways, have to be administered or managed. As long as there is management there will be the problem of how to manage better. In one sense, attempts at answers to the problem will be as numerous as there are managers, for each will bring his own individuality to the task. Nonetheless, at any one time there is enough in common for there to be broad similarities in what is thought and what is taught, and for this to be widely influenced by the views of writers past and present.

Among the best known are Frederick W. Taylor, Mary Parker Follett, Lyndall F. Urwick, E. F. L. Brech, Herbert A. Simon, Peter F. Drucker and Alfred P. Sloan Jr. Each of these in his or her own ways has sought to improve the understanding of administration and its practice. They have looked for the ingredients of a better management. Yet the contribution of each is distinctive.

Taylor's name is synonymous with the term 'scientific management'. His ideas made him a controversial figure in his own day and have remained a subject for argument. Mary Parker Follett's emphasis was on the 'law of the situation', which presents its own solutions if people will only look beyond the interplay of personalities. The British consultants Urwick and Brech have for many years collated and expounded general principles of administration, aiming at a unified body of knowledge. To Simon, however, the essence of management is the making of decisions, and he concentrates on analysing and improving the decision process. Drucker is concerned with establishing appropriate management by objectives, and Sloan, drawing on his experience at the head of the largest corporation in the world, with the management framework within which objectives are established and decisions made.

F. W. Taylor

Frederick Winslow Taylor (1856–1917) was an engineer by training. He joined the Midvale Steel Works as a labourer and rose rapidly to be foreman and later Chief Engineer. He was afterwards employed at the Bethlehem Steel Works, then became a consultant and devoted his time to the propagation of his ideas.

He first published his views on management in a paper entitled 'A piece rate system', read to the American Society of Mechanical Engineers in 1895. These views were expanded into a book *Shop Management* (1903) and further developed in *Principles of Scientific Management* (1911). As a result of labour troubles caused by the attempt to apply his principles in a government arsenal, a House of Representatives' Special Committee was set up in 1911 to investigate Taylor's system of shop management. (A full description of events at the arsenal is given in Aitken's case study.) In 1947, *Shop Management*, the *Principles*, and Taylor's Testimony to the Special Committee were collected together and published under the title of *Scientific Management*.

Taylor was the founder of the movement known as 'scientific management'. 'The principal object of management' he states, 'should be to secure the maximum prosperity for the employer, coupled with the maximum prosperity of each employee.' For the employer, 'maximum prosperity' means not just large profits in the short term but the development of all aspects of the enterprise to a state of permanent prosperity. For the employee 'maximum prosperity' means not just immediate higher wages, but his development so that he may perform efficiently in the highest grade of work for which his natural abilities fit him. The mutual interdependence of management and workers, and the necessity of their working together towards the common aim of increased prosperity for all seemed completely self-evident to Taylor. He was thus driven to asking why is there so much antagonism and inefficiency?

He suggests three causes: first, the fallacious belief of the workers that any increase in output would inevitably result in unemployment; second, the defective systems of management which make it necessary for each worker to restrict his output in order to protect his interests ('systematic soldiering'); third, inefficient rule-of-thumb effort-wasting methods of work. Taylor conceived it to be the aim of 'scientific management' to overcome these obstacles. This could be achieved by a systematic study of work to discover the most efficient methods of performing the job, and then a systematic study of management leading to the most efficient methods of controlling the workers. This would bring a great increase in efficiency and with it prosperity to the benefit of all, since a highly efficient prosperous business would be in a much better position to ensure the continuing well-paid employment of its workers. As Taylor put it: 'What the workmen want from their employers beyond anything else is high wages and what employers want from their workmen most of all is low labour cost of manufacture. . . . the existence or absence of these two elements forms the best index to either good or bad management.'

To achieve this Taylor lays down four 'great underlying principles of management':

The development of a true science of work

He points out that we do not really know what constitutes a fair day's work; a boss therefore has unlimited opportunities for complaining about his workers' inadequacies, and a worker never really knows what is expected of him. This can be remedied by the establishment after scientific investigation of a 'large daily task' as the amount to be done by a suitable worker under optimum conditions. For this he would receive a high rate of pay – much higher than the average worker would receive in 'unscientific' factories. He would also suffer a loss of income if he failed to achieve this performance.

The scientific selection and progressive development of the workman

To earn this high rate of pay a workman would have to be scientifically selected to ensure that he possesses the physical and intellectual qualities to enable him to achieve the output. Then he must be systematically trained to be a 'first-class' man. Taylor believes that every worker could be a first-class man at some job. It was the responsibility of management to develop workers, offering them opportunities for advancement which would finally enable them to do 'the highest, most interesting and most profitable class of work' for which they could become 'first-class' men.

The bringing together of the science of work and the scientifically selected and trained men

It is this process that causes the 'mental revolution' in management and Taylor maintains that almost invariably the major resistance to scientific management comes from the side of management. The workers, he finds, are very willing to cooperate in learning to do a good job for a high rate of pay.

The constant and intimate cooperation of management and men

There is an almost equal division of work and responsibility between management and workers. The management take over all the work for which they are better fitted than the workmen, i.e. the specification and verification of the methods, time, price and quality standards of the job, and the continuous supervision and control of the worker doing it. 'There is hardly a single act ... done by any workman in the shop which is not preceded by and followed by some act on the part of the men in management.' With this close personal cooperation the opportunities for conflict are almost eliminated, since the operation of this authority is not arbitrary.

The manager is continually demonstrating that his decisions are subject to the same discipline as the workmen, namely the scientific study of the work.

By 'science' Taylor means systematic observation and measurement, and an example of his method that he often quotes is the development of 'the science of shovelling'. He is insistent that, although shovelling is a very simple job, the study of the factors affecting efficient shovelling is quite complex. So much so that a man who is phlegmatic enough to be able to do the job and stupid enough to choose it, is extremely unlikely to be able to develop the most efficient method by himself. But this is in fact what is hoped will happen. The *scientific* study of shovelling involves the determination of the optimum load that a 'first-class man' can handle with each shovelful. Then the correct size of shovel to obtain this load, with different materials, must be established. Workers must be provided with a range of shovels and told which one to use. They must then be placed on an incentive payment scheme which allows first-class men to earn high wages (double what they would earn in 'unscientific' firms) in return for high production.

The insistence on maximum specialization, and the removal of all extraneous elements in order to concentrate on the essential task, is fundamental to Taylor's thinking. He applies this concept to management too. He considers that the work of a typical factory foreman is composed of a number of different functions (such as cost clerk, time clerk, inspector, repair boss, shop disciplinarian) and he believes that these could be separated out and performed by different specialists who would each be responsible for controlling different aspects of the work and the workers. He calls this system 'functional management' and likens the increased efficiency that it would bring to that obtained in a school where classes go to specialist teachers for different subjects, compared with a school in which one teacher teaches all subjects. He also formulates 'the exception principle' which lays down that management reports should be condensed into comparative summaries giving in detail only the exceptions to past standards or averages – both the especially good and the especially bad exceptions. Thus the manager would obtain an immediate and comprehensive view of the progress of his shop.

Taylor's methods have been followed by many others, among them Gantt, Frank and Lillian Gilbreth, Bedaux, Rowan and Halsey. They have developed his thinking into what is now called Work Study, or sometimes Industrial Engineering, a wider term. But even in his lifetime Taylor's ideas led to bitter controversy over the alleged inhumanity of his system, which was said to reduce men to the level of efficiently functioning machines. In fairness to Taylor, it must be said that his principles were often inadequately understood. For example, few managements have been willing to put into practice one of his basic tenets – that there should be no limit to the earnings of a high-producing worker; many incentive schemes involve such limits. This may inhibit the 'mental revolution' Taylor sought, which requires that 'both sides take their eyes off the division of the surplus as the all important matter and together turn their attention towards increasing the size of the surplus'.

Bibliography

Scientific Management, Harper & Row, 1947.

AITKEN, H. G. J., *Taylorism at Watertown Arsenal*, Harvard University Press, 1960.

Mary Parker Follett

Mary Parker Follett (1868–1933) was born in Boston and educated at Harvard and Cambridge. She was a student of philosophy, history and political science and wrote a number of works on political science including *The New State* and *Creative Experience*. In Boston she was very active in social work, taking a leading part in establishing evening classes and recreational centres for young people. She helped to develop youth employment bureaux and this led her to study industry and management. She gained a reputation as a writer and as an independent member of statutory wages boards. She spent most of the last five years of her life studying and lecturing in England. Her collected papers have been issued posthumously under the title *Dynamic Administration*.

Follett held very strongly that there are principles common to all spheres of administration. She became interested in business administration when she found that managers in industry were facing the same problems (of control, power, participation and conflict) as administrators in the public service. She felt that these problems were being more actively tackled by managers than by administrators. Business was a ferment of new ideas, and experiments were bolder.

Follett was interested in general questions about the working of organizations, of which the two most basic are: What do you want men to do, and how do you scientifically control and guide men's conduct in work and social relations? For answers to these questions she looked to an analysis of the fundamental motives involved in human relationships – particularly of the reactions of an individual within his social group. Her writings are an attempt to provide an outlook on management in which organization, leadership and power are dealt with as human problems. She was one of the first to appreciate the value of the then new tool of psychology. The problems for her are essentially those of reconciling individuals and social groups. Management must attempt to understand how these groups are formed and why, and how to weld them together into a community of aim and experience, so that the general purpose of the group is the common purpose of all its members.

Follett postulated four fundamental principles of organization:

Coordination by direct contact

The responsible people must be in direct contact regardless of their position in the organization. 'Horizontal' communication is as important as 'vertical' chains of command in achieving coordination.

Coordination in the early stages

The people concerned should be involved in policy or decisions while these are being formed and not simply brought in afterwards. In this way the benefits of participation will be obtained in increased motivation and morale.

Coordination as the 'reciprocal relating' of all factors in a situation

All factors have to be related to one another, and these interrelationships must themselves be taken into account.

Coordinating as a continuing process

'An executive decision is a moment in a process.' So many people contribute to the making of a decision that the concept of final or ultimate responsibility is an illusion. Combined knowledge and joint responsibility take its place. Authority and responsibility should derive from the actual function to be performed, not from place in the hierarchy.

It was Follett's belief that differences could be made to contribute to the common cause, if they were resolved not by domination or by compromise but by 'integration', so that from the conflict of ideas and attitudes a new advance towards the common objective emerged. She regarded as fundamental the joint study of facts and the bringing of objective differences into the open. From this would emerge the 'law of the situation' which would govern the orders to be given and the attitudes of groups and individuals to these orders. It is important to ensure that the work that people are required to do is based on the objective requirements of the situation – not on the personal whim of a particular manager. 'The head of the sales department does not give orders to the head of the production department, or vice versa. Each studies the market and the final decision is made as the market demands.'

Thus would be established an 'integrative unity' where each accepts responsibility for his particular contribution, to the best of his ability, and each fundamentally receives orders only from his own realization of what needs to be done. 'One *person* should not give orders to another *person*, but both should agree to take their orders from the situation.'

The idea of the organization as an 'integrative unity' may seem at variance with the traditional concepts of power, responsibility and leadership. Follett tries to show that these concepts, viewed in this new light, if anything strengthen the idea of unity. In the process, the notions of 'power *with*' rather than 'power *over*', of *joint* responsibility, and *multiple* leadership are developed. The leader must become aware of the group in which he works and must regard his job as being concerned with drawing out the abilities and contributions of individual members. He must know how 'to create a group power rather than express a personal power'.

The basis of Follett's thinking is the concept of partnership. The core of her contribution is the proposition that in a democratic society the primary task of management is so to arrange the situation that people cooperate readily of their own accord.

Bibliography

The New State, Longman, 1920.
Creative Experience, Longman, 1924.
Dynamic Administration, H. C. Metcalf and L. F. Urwick (eds.), Pitman, 1941.

L. F. Urwick and E. F. L. Brech

Lyndall F. Urwick (born 1891) has experience of both industry and the army, and was director of the International Management Institute in Geneva. Until 1951 he was head of a well-known firm of management consultants, and since then he has devoted himself to lecturing and writing about management. E. F. L. Brech has been a consultant colleague of Urwick and co-author with him of several books.

Both Urwick and Brech approach the subject of management in a manner similar to that of Fayol (see pp. 60–65). In Urwick's prolific books and booklets, Fayol's theoretical analysis and principles of application reappear continually. Indeed, the place of Urwick and Brech in the history of management is due less to innovations that either may have made in contemporary thinking than to their gathering of current ideas and the ideas of pioneers such as Fayol, Taylor (see pp. 97–101) and Follett (see pp. 102–4), and expounding them. Neither is associated with a particular line of argument. Both have striven to gain recognition for a broad range of principles of administration and so to develop a body of professional administrative knowledge.

Much of what Urwick has said and written on general management has been arranged under Fayol's headings of *forecasting, planning, organization, coordination, command* and *control*. In discussing these elements, Urwick has drawn together over the years a number of principles of good organization, founded on his conviction that a logical structure is better for efficiency and morale than one allowed to develop around personalities. For example, the *Principle of Specialization* states that as far as possible each individual should perform a single function only. This implies an increasingly specialized division of activities in industry, giving rise to three kinds of formal relations: 'line', 'functional' (where a department is responsible for a specialized function such as personnel or accounts), and 'staff'. Urwick strongly advocates the use of staff subordinates to help with the detailed work of coordination. These subordinates have staff relationships with other subordinates, in which they act not on their own authority but only on behalf of their chief.

Despite the complexity of highly specialized organizations, the *Principle of Authority* should be observed. There should be a clear line of authority, known and recognized, from the top to each individual. The duties, authority and responsibility of each position, and its relationships with other positions, should be defined in writing and made known to everyone concerned – the *Principle of Definition*. Moreover, in defining positions the *Principle of Correspondence* – authority being commensurate with responsibility – should be applied. The *Span of Control* of any manager should not exceed more than five, or at the most six, subordinates whose work interlocks. This is because he has to supervise not merely individual subordinates but the numerous interrelationships between them. So the maximum feasible span of control determines how far specialization can go by the addition of subordinates and may set a limit to delegation. Nevertheless, Urwick is of the opinion that managers overwhelmed with detail must blame their own failure to delegate.

But Urwick deals with far more than the structure of organization. He has a great deal to say on leadership, for instance. A leader should remember that there are four functions to his role: he embodies and represents the organization he serves; he initiates thought and action; he administers routine; and he interprets to others the purpose and meaning of what is done. Again, Urwick describes what makes a good plan for a business. He criticizes those who spend months choosing the right machine but imagine they have a flair for choosing the right man in an interview lasting a few minutes. He argues that superiors must take absolute responsibility for what their subordinates do. Indeed, there can be few topics in administration on which Urwick has not something to say.

E. F. L. Brech emphasizes management as a social process. To him, it is on the one hand a task of judgement and decision, and on the other the motivating of people to cooperative participation in carrying out the decisions reached. It is characteristic that he prefers to drop the word *command* from among the elements of management: he uses the term *motivation*.

Brech takes up and re-states most of Urwick's views, but in a way which brings them into line with current practice and attitudes. He does not always agree with Urwick. For example, in his opinion, a span of control need not necessarily be five or six; it will vary with the capacity of the manager concerned and the task. Some managers may find four subordinates too many, others may be able to carry eight or nine. Brech gives greater stress to management's responsibility for the personal and social satisfactions of its employees. And he believes that the morale of an organization is, in the end, largely a reflection of the outlook of its chief executive.

Between them, Urwick and Brech have surveyed the field of management so widely that nothing as succinct as this can do them justice. This, in fact, is the measure of their contribution.

Bibliography

The Making of Scientific Management, vol. 1: *Thirteen Pioneers;* vol. 2: *Management in British Industry;* vol. 3: *The Hawthorne Investigations*, Pitman, 1945–50.

URWICK, L. F., *The Elements of Administration*, Pitman, 1947.

BRECH, E. F. L., *Organization: The Framework of Management*, Longman, 1957.

URWICK, L. F., 'A short survey of industrial management' *B I M Occasional Papers*, 1962, no. 1, revised edn.

BRECH, E. F. L. (ed.), *The Principles and Practice of Management*, 2nd edn, Longman, 1963.

Herbert A. Simon

do not Reproduce

Herbert A. Simon is an American political and social scientist who began his career in local government. An early interest in the problems of evaluating the relative efficiency of different methods of local administration led him to the new field of 'operations research'. He is now Professor of Administration at Carnegie-Mellon University, and a consultant to government and business organizations. He also serves as director-at-large of the Social Science Research Council and director of the Nuclear Science and Engineering Corporation. Of recent years, Simon and his colleagues have been engaged in fundamental research into the processes of decision-making using electronic computers to simulate human thinking.

For Simon 'management' is equivalent to 'decision-making' and his major interest has been an analysis of how decisions are made and of how they might be made more effectively.

He describes three stages in the overall process of making a decision:

1. Finding occasions calling for a decision – the *intelligence* activity (using the word in the military sense);
2. Inventing, developing and analysing possible courses of action – the *design* activity;
3. Selecting a particular course of action from those available – the *choice* activity.

Generally speaking, intelligence activity precedes design, and design activity precedes choice; but the sequence of stages can be much more complex than this. Each stage in itself can be a complex decision-making process. The design stage can call for new intelligence activities. Problems at any stage can generate a series of sub-problems which in turn have their intelligence, design and choice stages. Nevertheless, in the process of organizational decision-making these three general stages can be discerned.

Carrying out the decisions is also regarded as a decision-making process. Thus after a policy decision has been taken, the executive having to carry it out is faced with a wholly new set of problems involving decision-making. Executing policy amounts to making more detailed policy. Essentially, for Simon, all managerial action is decision-making.

On what basis does the administrator make his decisions? The traditional theory of the economists assumed complete rationality. The 'model' was that of an 'economic man' who deals with the 'real world' in all its complexity, and who selects the rationally determined best course from among all those available to him in order to maximize his returns. But clearly this model is divorced from reality. We know that there is a large non-rational, emotional and unconscious element in man's thinking and behaviour. The need for an administrative theory is precisely because there are practical limits to human rationality. These limits to rationality are not static but depend upon the organizational environment in which the individual's decision takes place. It then becomes the task of administration, says Simon, 'so to design this environment that the individual will approach as close as practicable to rationality (judged in terms of the organization's goals) in his decisions'.

In place of 'economic man' Simon proposes a model of 'administrative man'. While economic man maximizes (i.e. selects the best course from those available to him), administrative man 'satisfices' – he looks for a course of action that is satisfactory or 'good enough'. In this process he is content with gross simplifications, taking into account only those comparatively few relevant factors which his mind can manage to encompass. 'Most human decision-making, whether individual or organizational, is concerned with the discovery and selection of satisfactory alternatives; only in exceptional cases is it concerned with the discovery and selection of optimal alternatives.' Most decisions are concerned not with searching for the sharpest needle in the haystack but with searching for a needle sharp enough to sew with. Thus administrative man can make decisions without searching for all the possible alternatives and can use relatively simple rules of thumb. In business terms he does not look for 'maximum profit' but 'adequate profit'; not 'optimum price' but 'fair price'. This makes his world much simpler.

What techniques of decision-making are then available? In discussing this problem, Simon makes a distinction between two polar types of decisions: *programmed* and *non-programmed* decisions. These are not mutually exclusive but rather make up a continuum stretching from highly programmed decisions at one end to highly unprogrammed decisions at the other. Decisions are programmed to the extent that they are repetitive and routine or a definite procedure has been worked out to deal with them. They thus do not have to be considered afresh each time they occur. Examples would be the decisions involved in processing a customer's order, determining an employee's sickness benefit or carrying out any routine job.

Decisions are unprogrammed to the extent that they are new and unstructured or where there is no cut-and-dried method for handling the problem. This may be either because it has not occurred before, or because it is particularly difficult or important. Examples would be decisions to introduce a new product, make substantial staff redundancies or move to a new location. All these decisions would be non-programmed (although entailing many programmed sub-decisions) because the organization would have no detailed strategy to govern its responses to these situations, and it would have to fall back on whatever general capacity it had for intelligent problem-solving.

Human beings are capable of acting intelligently in many new or difficult situations but they are likely to be less efficient. The cost to the organization of relying on non-programmed decisions in areas where special-purpose procedures and programmes can be developed is likely to be high and an organization should try to programme as many of its decisions as possible. The traditional techniques of programmed decision-making are habit, including knowledge and skills, clerical routines and standard operating procedures, and the organization's structure and culture, i.e. its system of common expectations, well-defined informational channels, established sub-goals, etc. The traditional techniques for dealing with non-programmed decisions rely on the selection and training of executives who possess judgement, intuition and creativity. These categories of technique have been developed over thousands of years (the building of the pyramids must have involved the use of many of them). But within the last decade, Simon argues, a complete revolution in techniques of decision-making has got under way, comparable to the invention of powered machinery in manufacture.

This revolution has been due to the application of such techniques as mathematical analysis, operational research, electronic data processing and computer simulation. These were used first for completely programmed operations (e.g. mathematical calculations, accounting procedures) formerly regarded as the province of clerks. But more and more elements of judgement (previously unprogrammed and the province of middle management) can now be incorporated into programmed procedures. Decisions on stock control and production control have been in the forefront of this development. With advances in computer technology, more and more complex decisions will become programmed. Even a completely unprogrammed decision, made once and for all, can be reached via computer techniques by building a model of the decision situation. Various courses of action can then be simulated and their effects assessed. 'The automated factory of the future', Simon maintains, 'will operate on the basis of programmed decisions produced in the automated office beside it.'

Bibliography

Administrative Behaviour, 2nd edn, Macmillan Co., 1960.
The New Science of Management Decision, Harper & Row, 1960.
The Shape of Automation, Harper & Row, 1965.

MARCH, J. G., and SIMON, H. A., *Organizations*, Wiley, 1958.

Peter F. Drucker

Peter Drucker was born in Austria where he qualified in law in 1931. He was on the editorial staff of the *Frankfurter General Anzeiger* until the advent of the Nazis. After a period in London he moved to New York in 1937. He was initially a correspondent for a group of British papers, then an economic consultant for a number of banks and insurance companies. He became an adviser on business policy and management to a number of large American corporations. His books are based on his varied consultancy work over the past three decades.

Drucker's work begins with a view of top management and its critical role in the representative institution of modern industrial society, namely the large corporation. Following from this he identifies management as the central problem area, and the manager as the dynamic element in every business. It is the manager through his control of the decision-making structure of the modern corporation who breathes life into the organization and the society. The manager is given human and material resources to work with, and from them he fashions a productive enterprise from which springs the wealth of the society. This is becoming increasingly true as we move into an era of knowledge technology, making human resources ever more central to effective performance in organizations. Yet as Drucker points out, managers, while becoming ever more basic resources of a business, are increasingly the scarcest, the most expensive and the most perishable. Given this, it becomes extremely important that managers should be used as effectively as is possible at the present state of knowledge about the practice and functions of management. It is to the problem of managerial effectiveness that Drucker addresses himself.

It is only possible to arrive at prescriptions for effectiveness if we first understand the role of the manager in the organization; if we know what the job of management is. There are, says Drucker, two dimensions to the task of management, an economic dimension and a time dimension. Managers are responsible for business organizations (this distinguishes them from administrators generally). As such they must always put economic performance first; the final standard for judging them is economic performance, which of course is not the case for all administrators. The second dimension, time, is one which is present in all decision-making systems. Management always has to think of the impact of a decision on the present, the short-term future and the long-term future. This is, of course, tied in with the economic aspect. Taken together it means that managers are evaluated in terms of their economic performance in the present, the short-term and the long-term.

Management, then, is the job of organizing resources to achieve satisfactory performance; to produce an enterprise from material and human resources. According to Drucker this does not necessarily mean profit maximization. For him profit is not the cause of business behaviour, or the rationale of business decision-making in the sense of always attempting to achieve the maximum profit. Rather profit is a test of the validity or success of the business enterprise. The aim of any business is to achieve sufficient profit, which will cover the risks that have been taken and avoid a loss.

The central question for Drucker is how best to manage a business to ensure that profits are made, and that the enterprise is successful over time. Although it is possible to state the overall aims in a fairly precise and simple way, any on-going functioning organization has a variety of needs and goals. It is not realistic to think of an enterprise having a single objective. Efficient management always involves a juggling act, balancing the different possible objectives, deciding the priorities to be put on the multiple aims that an organization has. Because of this, and due to the complex nature of business as exemplified by departmentalization, management by objectives is vital. This is essential in the process of ensuring that informed judgement takes place. It forces managers to examine available alternatives and provides a reliable means for evaluating management performance.

Specifically, objectives in a business enterprise enable management to explain, predict and control activities in a way which single ideas like profit maximization do not. First, they enable the organization to explain the whole range of business phenomena in a small number of general statements. Secondly, they allow the testing of these statements in actual experience. Thirdly, it becomes possible to predict behaviour. Fourthly, the soundness of decisions can be examined while they are still being made rather than after the fact. Fifthly, performance in the future can be improved as a result of the analysis of past experience. This is because objectives force one to plan in detail what the business must aim at and to work out ways of effectively achieving these aims. Management by objectives involves spelling out what is meant by managing a business. By doing this, and then examining the outcome over time the five advantages outlined above are realized.

But this still leaves the problem of what the objectives of a business enterprise should be. To quote Drucker: 'Objectives are needed in every area where performance and results directly and vitally affect the survival and prosperity of the business.' More concretely, there are eight areas in business where performance objectives must be set. These areas are: market standing; innovation; productivity; physical and financial resources; profitability; manager performance and development; worker performance and attitude; public responsibility. In deciding how to set objectives for these areas it is necessary to take account of possible measures and lay down a realistic time span. Measures are important because they make things visible and 'real'; they tell the manager what to focus his attention upon. Unfortunately measurement in most areas of business is still at a very crude level. As far as the time span of objectives is concerned, this depends on the area and the nature of the business. In the lumber business, today's plantings are the production capacity of fifty years' time; in parts of the clothing industry a few weeks' time may be the 'long range future'.

But perhaps the most important part of management by objectives is the effect that it has on the manager himself. It enables the organization to develop its most important resource, management. This is because managerial self-control is developed, leading to stronger motivation and more efficient learning. It is the essence of this style of management that each manager arrives at a set of realistic objectives for the unit which he controls, and for himself. These objectives should spell out the contribution that the manager will make to the attainment of company goals in all areas of the business. It is always necessary that the objectives set should be checked by higher levels of management to make sure that they are attainable (neither too high nor too low). But the importance of individual managerial involvement in the setting of objectives cannot be overstressed as a motivator. If the manager is really going to be able to develop himself in performance terms and take proper advantage of the system, he must be given information direct which will enable him to measure his own performance. This is very different from the situation in some companies where certain groups (e.g. accountants) act as the 'secret police' of the chief executive.

The necessity of individual managers setting their own objectives stems from the nature of modern business, and what Drucker calls three forces of misdirection. These are, the specialized work of most managers, the existence of a hierarchy, and the differences in vision that exist in businesses. All these raise the possibility of breakdowns and conflicts in the organization. Management by objectives is a way of overcoming these deficiencies by relating the task of each manager to the overall goals of the company. By doing this it takes note of an important aspect of modern business operations; management is no longer the domain of one man. Even the chief executive does not operate in isolation. Management is a group operation, and the existence of objectives emphasizes the contribution that each individual manager makes to the total group operation. The problem of a chief executive is that of picking the best managerial group; the existence of objectives with their built-in evaluation system enables better choices to be made.

Management by objectives, then, enables an executive to be effective. An important point is that effectiveness can be learned. Drucker insists that the self-development of effective executives is central to the continued development of the organization as the 'knowledge worker' becomes the major resource. The system of objectives allows the manager to evaluate his performance and by so doing strengthens the learning process. This is done by showing where the particular strengths of the individual are, as a result of which he can make these strengths productive by demonstrating the correctness of different systems of priorities, and by producing effective decision-making patterns. The regular review of objectives and performance enables the manager to know where his most effective contribution is made, how it is made, and as a result develop his skills in these areas.

Overall then, management by objectives helps to overcome some of the forces which threaten to split the organization by clearly relating the task of each manager to the overall aims of the company. It allows learning to take place and as a result the development of each manager to the best of his capacities. And finally, and most importantly, it increases the motivation of the managers and develops their commitment to the organization. The result is that organizational goals are reached by having common people achieve uncommon performance.

Bibliography

The Practice of Management, Harper & Row, 1954.
Managing for Results, Harper & Row, 1964.
The Effective Executive, Harper & Row, 1966.

Alfred P. Sloan Jr

Alfred Sloan (1875–1966) spent forty-five years in the General Motors Corporation of America, the largest industrial corporation in the world. For twenty-three of those years, from 1923 until 1946, he was the chief executive officer of the corporation and he continued as Chairman of the Board until 1956. As such he was the person with the greatest influence on the way in which General Motors developed. He was largely responsible for the creation of the present form of the organization and of the methods of its top management, and through this achievement has had a considerable influence on the methods of management of many large industrial and other enterprises, whose developments are analysed in Chandler's study.

Sloan, an engineer by training, was the epitome of the professional manager. In this he contrasted very strongly with the founder of General Motors, William Durant, who had a highly personal style of management akin to his great rival in the American motor industry, Henry Ford. Durant was a genius at creating enterprises but was much less capable of carrying them on, and a bankers' trust and later the du Pont Company acquired control before General Motors became financially independent. Sloan, on the other hand, although he had a considerable fortune by personal standards (now administered by the Sloan Foundation), never at its greatest owned more than one per cent of the stock of the corporation. He was thus in Weber's terms (see p. 20) the bureaucratic administrator who succeeded the charismatic founder. In 1963 Sloan published *My Years with General Motors* in which he gave a history of the top management problems of the Corporation and his methods of handling them. In this he demonstrated the way in which the technical, financial, organizational and personal factors interact in the management of large enterprises.

The recurrent theme of Sloan's book is the necessity of dealing with the major problem which faces any large multi-operation enterprise: the appropriate degree of centralization or decentralization of authority for decisions. The centralizing approach has the advantages of flexibility and perhaps speed, but places an enormous weight on the top man. He may be a genius in many of his decisions, but he will also be haphazard, irrational and apathetic in regard to others. This was the Henry Ford approach. The decentralizing approach has the advantage of allowing decisions to be made closer to the operational bases of the enterprise, but runs the real danger that decisions will be taken with regard to the best interests of the particular operating division itself without concern for the best interests of the corporation as a whole. This was the William Durant method. He brought many companies into the General Motors Corporation (including the roller bearing company owned by Sloan) and allowed their managements to operate much as before with little regard to the rather nebulous concept of the corporation as a whole. The management history of General Motors is one of the attempt to find the right balance between these two extremes, in an industrial environment of constant change and continuous, but fluctuating, growth.

A nice example of the extreme decentralization in the early days is the description given by Sloan of the method of cash control. Each operating unit controlled its own cash, depositing all receipts in its own accounts and paying all bills from them. There was no income directly to the Corporation and no effective procedure for getting cash from the points where it happened to be to the points where it was needed. When the Corporation needed cash to pay dividends, taxes and other charges, the treasurer had to request cash from the operating divisions. But the divisions wanted to keep as much cash as possible to satisfy their own peak requirements and their financial staff were highly adept at delaying the reporting of cash in hand. The treasurer would thus have to guess how much cash a division had in hand and decide how much of this he would try to get from them. He would visit them, discuss other general matters and then casually at the end of the conversation bring up the topic of cash. The division would always express surprise at the amount that he wanted, and occasionally would try to resist the transfer of such a large amount. The effects of this bargaining situation were that over the Corporation as a whole funds were not efficiently utilized, and so a centralized cash control system was set up. General Motors Corporation accounts were established and controlled by the central finance staff; all receipts were credited to them and all payments made from them. Transfers between one account and another could be made quickly and easily across the whole country when cash needed in one place was available in another. Minimum and maximum balances for each local account were set, intercorporation settlements were facilitated, and forward planning of cash was developed, all by the central staff.

So centralization can clearly bring great advantages, and systems of coordination for purchasing, corporate advertising, engineering and so on were set up. But there is also a clear need for decentralization if the central directing staff is not to stifle the division managements. The controversy over the 'copper-cooled engine' which rent the Corporation in the early nineteen-twenties well illustrates this. The research section of the central staff had developed a revolutionary air-cooled engine and with the strong backing of the then Chairman, Pierre du Pont, was pressing that all production should be turned over to this type. The operating divisions were resistant since they regarded the development as unproven on a production and use basis. Sloan did not regard himself as technically competent to take a view on the merits of the engine, but from a purely managerial analysis he came to the conclusion that for the central direction of the corporation to force the change on unwilling division managements would be in effect for them to undertake the operating management of the divisions – a degree of centralization which was inappropriate and basically unworkable. He therefore threw his weight in support of the divisions, proposing that a special subsidiary of the research division be formed to develop and manufacture cars based on the new engine. This was done, and, although the development eventually proved unworkable with the engineering technology of those days, the Corporation learnt a great deal from this controversy about the correct balance between the centre and the divisions.

Top management, according to Sloan, has the basic tasks of providing motivation and opportunity for its senior executives; motivation by incentive compensation through stock option plans, and opportunity through decentralized management. But coordination is also required, and good management rests on a reconciliation of centralization and decentralization. It was through his attempts to obtain the correct structural balance between these extremes, that Sloan enunciated his seemingly paradoxical principle of 'coordinated decentralization'. His aim was coordinated control of decentralized operations. Policy coordination is achieved through committees. It is evolved in a continuous debate to which all may contribute, and is basically an educational process. Executive administration is the clear responsibility of individuals who carry out the evolving policy. Many policy groups were established in the Corporation, but none of them detracted from the executive functions – indeed they are the means of controlling them.

For such a system of coordinated control of decentralized operations to work, one further element is needed – committees have to be supplied with adequate facts on which to base policies, and executive management has to be based on fact. Time and time again throughout his tenure of office Sloan emphasized this; debates are being conducted on conjectures, decisions are taken on superficial evidence, only inadequate information is available and improved systems must be developed to correct this. Through his influence General Motors pioneered many new techniques for obtaining managerially relevant information, particularly in financial control through the use of return on capital as a measure of efficiency, and in the statistical forecasting of market demand.

Bibliography

My Years with General Motors, Sidgwick & Jackson, 1965.

CHANDLER, A. D., *Strategy and Structure*, MIT Press, 1962.

4 People in Organizations

Management succeeds or fails in proportion as it is accepted without reservation by the group as authority and leader.
Elton Mayo

Psycho-economic equilibrium is best achieved in the individual by a level of work corresponding to his capacity, and equitable payment for that work.
Elliott Jaques

It is my hypothesis that the present organizational strategies developed and used by administrators (be they industrial, educational, religious, governmental or trade union) lead to human and organizational decay. It is also my hypothesis that this need not be so.
Chris Argyris

The primary functions of any organization, whether religious, political or industrial, should be to implement the needs of man to enjoy a meaningful existence.
Frederick Herzberg

The entire organization must consist of a multiple overlapping group structure with *every* work group using group decision-making processes skillfully.
Rensis Likert

The average human being learns, under proper conditions, not only to accept but to seek responsibility.
Douglas McGregor

The 9, 9 orientation to the management of production and people aims at integrating these two aspects of work under conditions of high concern for both.
R. R. Blake and J. S. Mouton

Organizations are systems of interdependent *human beings*. Although this has been recognized implicitly by many of the writers of the previous chapters, and explicitly by some, their main concern has been with the 'formal system' – its aims, the principles on which it should be constituted to achieve them, and the methods by which it should function. People have then been considered as one of the essential resources required to achieve the aims. But people are a rather special sort of resource. They not only work for the organization – they *are* the organization.

The behaviour of the members of an organization clearly affects both its structure and its functioning, as well as the principles on which it can be managed. Most importantly, human beings affect the aims of organizations in which they participate – not merely the methods used to accomplish them. The writers in this chapter are social scientists who are specifically concerned to analyse the behaviour of people and its effects on all aspects of the organization. They have studied human attitudes, expectations, value systems, tensions and conflicts and the effects these have on productivity, adaptability, cohesion and morale. They have regarded the organization as a 'natural system' – an organism whose processes have to be studied in their own right – rather than as a 'formal system' – a mechanism designed to achieve particular ends.

Elton Mayo is the founding father of the 'Human Relations Movement' which brought into prominence the view that workers and managers must first be understood as human beings. Elliott Jaques has focused upon the problems of tension and lessening them through adequate role definition and equitable payment. Chris Argyris has been concerned to examine and control the inevitable conflict between the needs of the individual and the needs of the organization, and Frederick Herzberg to determine how the characteristically human needs of man for growth and development may be satisfied in work.

Rensis Likert and Douglas McGregor reject the underlying assumptions about human behaviour on which formal organizations have been built and propose new methods of management based on a more adequate understanding of human motivation, while Robert Blake and Jane Mouton describe a form of management which shows equal high concern for both production and people.

Elton Mayo
and the Hawthorne Investigations

Elton Mayo (1880–1949) was an Australian who spent most of his working life at Harvard University, eventually becoming Professor of Industrial Research in the Graduate School of Business Administration. In this post he was responsible for the initiation and direction of many research projects, the most famous being the five-year investigation of the Hawthorne works of the Western Electric Company in Chicago. Immediately prior to his death, Mayo was consultant on industrial problems to the British Government.

Elton Mayo has often been called the founder of both the Human Relations movement and of industrial sociology. The research that he directed showed the importance of groups in affecting the behaviour of individuals at work and enabled him to make certain deductions about what managers ought to do.

Like most of his contemporaries, Mayo's initial interests were in fatigue, accidents and labour turnover, and the effect on these of rest pauses and physical conditions of work. One of his first investigations was of a spinning mill in Philadelphia where labour turnover in one department was 250 per cent compared with an average of 6 per cent for all the other departments. Rest pauses were introduced by Mayo and production and morale improved. When the operatives took part in fixing the frequency and duration of the pauses a further improvement was registered and morale in the whole factory also improved. At the end of the first year, turnover in the department concerned was down to the average for the rest of the mill. The initial explanation was that the rest pauses, in breaking up the monotony of the job, improved the mental and physical condition of the men. However, after subsequent investigations, Mayo modified his explanation.

The major investigation which led to this modification and which laid the basis for a great many subsequent studies was the Hawthorne Experiment carried out between 1927 and 1932. Prior to the entry of Mayo's team an inquiry had been made by a number of engineers into the effect of illumination on the worker and his work. Two groups of workers had been isolated and the lighting conditions for one had been varied and for the other held constant. No significant differences in output were found between the two; indeed whatever was done with the lighting, production rose in *both* groups.

At this point the Industrial Research team directed by Mayo took over. The first stage of their inquiry is known as the Relay Assembly Test Room. Six female operatives, engaged in assembling telephone relays, were segregated in order to observe the effect on output and morale of various changes in the conditions of work. During five years of experiment various changes were introduced and a continuous record of output was kept. At first a special group payment scheme was introduced: previously the girls had been grouped with one hundred other operatives for incentive payment purposes. Other changes introduced at various times were rest pauses in several different forms (varying the length and spacing), shorter hours and refreshments, in all more than ten changes. Before putting the changes into effect, the investigators spent a lot of time discussing them with the girls. Communication between the workers and the research team was very full and open throughout the experimental period. Almost without exception output increased with each change made.

The next stage in the experiment was to return to the original conditions. The operatives reverted to a forty-eight-hour six-day week, no incentives, no rest pauses and no refreshment. Output went up to the highest yet recorded. By this time it had become clear, to quote Mayo, 'that the itemized changes experimentally imposed . . . could not be used to explain the major change – the continually increasing production'. The explanation eventually given was that the girls experienced a tremendous increase in work satisfaction because they had greater freedom in their working environment and control over their own pace-setting. The six operatives had become a social group with their own standards and expectations. By removing the girls from the normal setting of work and by intensifying their interaction and cooperation, informal practices, values, norms and social relationships had been built up giving the group high cohesion. Also, the communication system between the researchers and the workers was extremely effective; this meant that the norms of output were those that the girls felt the researchers desired. The supervisors took a personal interest in each girl and showed pride in the record of the group. The result was that the workers and the supervisors developed a sense of participation and as a result established a completely new working pattern. Mayo's generalization was that work satisfaction depends to a large extent on the informal social pattern of the work group. Where norms of cooperativeness and high output are established because of a feeling of importance, physical conditions have little impact.

However, this is the explanation arrived at in later years. At the time of the actual experiment, the continually increasing output was regarded as something of a mystery so an inquiry was instituted into conditions in the factory at large. This took the form of an interview programme. It was quickly realized that such a programme told the researchers little about the actual conditions in the factory but a great deal about the attitudes of various employees. The major finding of this stage of the inquiry was that many problems of worker–management cooperation were the results of the emotionally based attitudes of the workers rather than of objective difficulties in the situation. Workers, thought Mayo, were activated by a 'logic of sentiment', whereas management is concerned with the 'logic of cost and efficiency'. Conflict is inevitable unless this difference is understood and provided for.

The third stage of the investigation was to observe a group performing a task in a natural setting, i.e. a non-experimental situation. A number of employees in what became known as the Bank Wiring Observation Room were under constant observation and their output recorded. It was found that they restricted their output; the group had a standard for output and this was not exceeded by any individual. The attitude of the members of the group towards the company's financial incentive scheme was one of indifference. The group was highly integrated with its own social structure and code of behaviour which clashed with that of management. Essentially this code was composed of solidarity on the part of the group against management. Not too much work should be done, that would be ratebusting; on the other hand, not too little work should be done, that would be chiselling. There was little recognition of the organization's formal allocation of roles. This was confirmation of the importance of informal social groupings in determining levels of output.

Taken as a whole, the significance of the Hawthorne investigation was in 'discovering' the informal organization which it is now realized exists in all organizations. It demonstrated the importance to individuals of stable social relationships in the work situation. It confirmed Mayo in his wider thinking that what he calls the 'rabble hypothesis' about human behaviour (that each individual pursues his own rational self-interest) was completely false. It confirmed his view that the breakdown of traditional values in society could be countered by creating a situation in industry conducive to spontaneous cooperation. For Mayo, one of the major tasks of management is to organize spontaneous cooperation, thereby preventing the further breakdown of society. As traditional attachments to community and family disappear, and as the workplace increases in importance, the support given by traditional institutions must now be given by the organization. Conflict, competition and disagreement between individuals is to be avoided by management understanding its role as providing the basis for group affiliation. From the end of the Hawthorne project to his death Mayo was interested in discovering how spontaneous cooperation could be achieved. It is this which has been the basis of the Human Relations movement, the use of the insights of the social sciences to secure the commitment of individuals to the ends and activities of the organization.

Elliott Jaques
and the Glacier Investigations

Elliott Jaques is a Canadian who graduated in psychology at the University of Toronto and later in medicine at the Johns Hopkins Medical School. After service in the Royal Canadian Army Medical Corps, he joined the staff of the Tavistock Institute of Human Relations, where over a period of years he led a study of worker and management activities in the Glacier Metal Company – an engineering factory in London whose managing director was Wilfred Brown (see pp. 71–4). This series of investigations may well come to bear comparison with the Hawthorne Studies for their impact on management thinking. For this work he was awarded a Doctorate of Philosophy in the Department of Social Relations at Harvard University. Jaques is a qualified psychoanalyst and in recent years has been working as an independent consultant – partly as a psychotherapist in private practice and partly as 'social therapist' to the Glacier Company. In 1965 he was appointed Professor of Social Sciences at Brunel University, London.

Jaques and his collaborators in the Glacier Investigations use the technique of 'action research'. They work in collaboration with members of the firm to study psychological and social forces affecting group behaviour; to develop more effective ways of resolving social stress; and to facilitate agreed and desired social change.

The problems they tackle are those on which particular groups in the organization request their help. Thus Jaques's book *The Changing Culture of a Factory* describes, for example, studies of problems of payment and morale in the Service Department, worker–management cooperation in the Works Committee, executive leadership at the Divisional Managers' meeting. The method used consists of the 'working-through' (by the investigator and the group together) of current problems and their possible solutions. The investigator attends meetings of the group, and interprets to it the social and personal factors at play in an attempt to increase the social and psychological insight of the group. This also promotes a more rational attitude to social change.

The 'working-through' process usually leads to the discovery that the apparent problems of the group are only symptoms of more basic and long-term difficulties and these are then examined. What began as an issue of wages and methods of payment in the Service Department, for example, soon developed into the complex ramifications of inter-group stresses so often associated with wage questions. As a result of the working-through of management and worker differences at a series of meetings of representatives of both sides (which was facilitated by the investigator's interpretations), not only was the change-over to a new system of payment accomplished, but in the new situation created by these discussions it was possible to institute a Shop Council as a continuing mechanism through which members could take part in setting policy for the department.

One of the most important findings to come out of the Glacier investigations is the individual's felt need to have his role and status clearly defined in a way which is acceptable both to himself and to his colleagues. Where there is some confusion of role boundaries, or where multiple roles occupied by the same person are not sufficiently distinguished, insecurity and frustration result. The study of the Divisional Managers' meeting showed that it functioned sometimes as an executive management committee taking decisions for the London factory, sometimes as a group for non-decision-making discussions with the Managing Director, and sometimes as a concealed Board of Directors for the whole company (including the Scottish factory). In this mixture of different functions, the same group had different powers over the affairs of the organization, depending on the particular capacity in which it was functioning. But these powers were not clear and this was personally disturbing to the members.

Even when a role has been defined it may contain elements which the individual finds unacceptable or difficult to fill. In an organization committed to consultative management, a superior may become increasingly unwilling to exercise his authority. Jaques describes some mechanisms by which he may avoid responsibility and authority. One is the exercise of a consultative relationship only. Thus the Managing Director failed to perceive that he also held a role as chief executive of the London factory, and adopted only a consultative Managing Director's role to the Divisional Managers. This left a gap in the executive hierarchy. Another mechanism is the misuse of the process of formal joint consultation. This often provides an escape route from accepting responsibility for immediate subordinates, by making possible easy and direct contact between higher management and workers' representatives. Thus to make consultative management work, the consultation must follow the chain of command; otherwise conflict arises from those by-passed. Yet another evasive possibility is pseudo-democracy: a superior asserting 'I'm just an ordinary member of this committee' when he is in fact the senior person present; or a superior avoiding the leadership role by excessive delegation. One of the most important conclusions is that there is a distinctive leadership role in groups that members expect to be properly filled; and groups do not function well unless it is.

At the conclusion of these Tavistock studies, Jaques changed his position, becoming, with the consent of the workers' representatives, a part-time employee of the firm. He still retained his independent position, however, and continued his role as 'social analyst', working on problems of wages and salaries. Previous discussion had revealed continuous problems arising from supposed unfair differences in pay, and the task was to determine the appropriate payment and status of individuals. How can one establish what will be generally accepted as the right level of pay for a given job, particularly in relation to other jobs?

Work was divided by Jaques into its prescribed and its discretionary content. Prescribed work is specified in such a way as to leave nothing to the judgement of the individual doing it. But *all* jobs have some content, however small, which requires the individual to use discretion. From this developed the concept of the 'time span of discretion' – the idea that the main criterion by which the importance of a job is implicitly evaluated is the length of time which expires before decisions taken by an individual are reviewed and evaluated. At the lowest level what the individual does is frequently checked, but at the highest level it might take several years before the effectiveness of a decision shows up. This approach is developed by Jaques in *The Measurement of Responsibility*.

From later work, described in *Equitable Payment*, he puts forward a general theory of work, differential payment and individual progress, based on three separate analytical measurements. These are the time-span of discretion, the equitable work-payment scale, which relates a person's payment to the range of level of work in his job, and the standard earning progression curves, which relate to the growth in capacity of the individual. Attention can be focused on the norms which people have about equitable payment in society, and by the use of these objective tools of analysis inequities can be remedied, with consequent gain in social cohesion. Jaques believes that an individual functions best when working at a level which corresponds to his capacity at his normal pace and intensity of application, and when he obtains equitable payment for that work.

Bibliography

The Changing Culture of a Factory, Tavistock, 1951.
The Measurement of Responsibility, Tavistock, 1956.
Equitable Payment, Heinemann, 1961; Penguin, 1967.

BROWN, W., and JAQUES, E., *Glacier Project Papers*, Heinemann, 1965.

Chris Argyris

For many years Professor of Industrial Administration at Yale University, Chris Argyris took his first degree in psychology. He has consistently studied how the personal development of the individual is affected by the kind of situation in which that individual works. Argyris sees each individual person as having a potential which can be fully realized. Such self-realization, or self-actualization, benefits not only the individual but also those around him and the organization in which he works. Unfortunately, business and other organizations are usually run in a way which positively prevents any such benefits.

There are three sides to this problem. They are the development of the individual towards personal or psychological maturity, the degree of interpersonal competence in dealing with one another shown by those with whom he works, and the nature of the organization for which he works.

Fundamentally, what an adult does at work can be understood by the extent to which he has matured from the infantile ways of babyhood. This progression from infancy towards maturity may be said to consist of seven developments:

1. From infant passivity towards adult activity.
2. From dependence towards relative independence.
3. From limited behaviours to many different behaviours.
4. From erratic, shallow, brief interests to more stable, deeper interests.
5. From short time perspective to longer time perspective.
6. From a subordinate social position to an equal or super-ordinate social position.

7. From lack of self-awareness to self-awareness and self-control.

A young child's interests and enjoyments shift from minute to minute, and he is concerned only with here and now – he cannot wait till later for his ice-cream. He is self-centred and unaware of how his demands affect others: but he accepts a dependent position in which others largely control what he does. Mature adulthood is achieved when the individual has some ability to see himself from the point of view of others, to foresee consequences even years ahead, to pursue interests consistently, and to accept responsibilities equal to or superior to those of others.

With such development goes the possibility for the full and constructive release of psychological energy. Each individual has a set of needs, and if offered potential satisfaction and yet some challenge in the process, will put all his energies into meeting the challenge.

The trouble is that the typical approach to the management of organizations, and the lack of interpersonal competence in them, prevent people becoming mature in outlook and fail to arouse their full psychological energy. People too often remain short-sighted in their actions on the job, concerned with present advantage and unable to see future consequences; they shirk responsibility and are uninterested in opportunities; their approach to their work is apathetic. But the fault is not theirs individually.

In factories, in research organizations, in hospitals, among executives, among scientists, among technicians, on the shop floor, everywhere, Argyris' research suggests that interpersonal competence is low. That is, people find excuses for what they do, or don't stop to notice its effects on others; they only half hear what others try to tell them; they stick to their habitual ways and never try a new approach to someone else. The results are mutual suspicion and distrust, a tendency to avoid telling everything to the other person, and a reluctance in being honest about one's own feelings or those of the other person. In such a situation, people show a superficial 'pseudo-health' in which although there is no active dissatisfaction, each confines himself to his minimum routine tasks in an indifferent manner, and refuses to look any further than these. True frankness of manner and commitment to the job are missing.

This atmosphere is common in organizations which are not 'axiologically good'. The term 'axiologically good' describes an organization which *is* an organization as that word is usually defined, i.e. all its parts are well coordinated and inter-related to further the overall objectives, and it is able to respond to internal and external needs for change. Anything which is not like this would be better described as a non-organization which does not have the essential properties of organization. Often these properties are indeed absent. Formal 'rational' organization is based on reducing tasks to minimal specialized routines. Its principles include a chain of command by which people doing such tasks can be directed and controlled, through a series of managers and supervisors. The concern is with spans of control (number of subordinates to each superordinate) and with instructions. As a result its constituent specialists and departments follow their own ends irrespective of wider interests and even to each other's detriment.

In such organizations the individual cannot progress from infantile behaviours. In his limited routine task he looks forward to the end of the day's work, but is unable to foresee the success or failure of the whole organization over a period of years. To his superiors his infuriating inability to see beyond the end of his nose is inexplicable. His concerns are restricted to his own relatively trivial work difficulties, and he is not at first interested in the chance of anything more than this. He comes to accept a passive and dependent position, without initiative.

Faced with this lack of response, even among lower managers or specialists, executives are liable to become yet more autocratic and directive. Their existing strong 'pyramidal values' are reinforced. The increased use of management controls deprives employees of any opportunity of participating in the important decisions which affect their working life, leading to feelings of psychological failure. It is not they themselves but control systems (such as work study and cost accounting) which define, inspect and evaluate the quality and quantity of their performance. And as subordinates tell less and less about what is happening, as everyone pays more attention to keeping up appearances ready for the next job study investigation or tense budget allocation committee meeting, so less effort goes into the job itself.

Effective management must aim at the full development of individual potentialities, at 'authentic' and open interpersonal relationships, and at coherent organization. Greater commitment of psychological energy by individuals and better coordination between everyone leads to more effective performance by the whole organization.

'The first step towards increasing organizational health is for the top to increase its interpersonal competence.' Top managers must not be afraid to show their real feelings to those above and below them. They must try to speak constructively about one another in a way which is honest and helpful ('descriptive non-evaluative feedback'). They must refuse to become defensive about what other people think. This approach will then spread through the organization, reducing tension and concealed criticism.

Jobs can be 'enlarged', not merely to include more operations of the same low level, but to expand the use of the individual's intellectual and interpersonal abilities. Wherever possible greater responsibility is included for handling problems, for quality, for thinking ahead, rather than taking such responsibilities away to controlling inspectors, supervisors, and specialists. Each employee can have more control over what is done in his own sphere of activities, and greater participation in decisions about them. Information is used to help people do the job and is evaluated by those whom it concerns, rather than being used to 'check up on' and discipline them.

The organization itself will change. Looking to the future, organizations may be capable of rapid adaptation, to the point where they have different structures for different purposes. Each structure will have different mixes of character-istics. One mix may approximate what has been called 'axiolo-gically good' organization, similar to organic organization (see Burns, p. 45): another is the participative structure advocated by Likert (see p. 147) or the defined but consultative structure emerging from the Glacier Metal projects (see Brown p. 72 and Jaques p. 132). This latter should not be abandoned: it may be very appropriate when time is short for decision and action. The point is that the human costs of using it should be recognized. On the other hand, when there is time for discus-sion and consideration and maximum personal responsibility is desired, the organic strategy can be used. 'If one asks in the organization of the future to see the company organizational chart, he will be asked: "For what type of decision?".' This view cuts through the debate about delegation versus centrali-zation. Each is appropriate to different conditions and problems.

Argyris believes that the training and detachment of the social scientist enable him to help people to understand themselves and their situation at work. In his latest book he describes how a change agent may most effectively help to achieve such understanding and to encourage the appropriate action which flows from it.

Bibliography

Personality and Organization, Harper & Row, 1957.
Understanding Organizational Behaviour, Tavistock, 1960.
Interpersonal Competence and Organizational Effectiveness, Tavistock, 1962.
Integrating the Individual and the Organization, Wiley, 1964.
Organization and Innovation, Irwin, 1965.
Intervention Theory and Method, Addison-Wesley, 1970.

Frederick Herzberg

Frederick Herzberg is Professor and Chairman of Psychology at Western Reserve University, Cleveland. For over a decade he has been concerned with his colleagues in a programme of research and application on human motivation in the work situation and its effects on the individual's psychological growth and mental health. Like Argyris (see p. 135) he questions whether the current methods of organizing work in business and industry are appropriate for man's total needs and happiness.

Herzberg and his colleagues conducted a survey of two hundred engineers and accountants representing a cross-section of Pittsburgh industry. These men were asked to remember times when they felt exceptionally good about their jobs. The investigators probed for the reasons why they felt as they did, asking for a description of the sequence of events which gave that feeling. The questions were then repeated for sequences of events which made them feel exceptionally bad about their jobs. The responses were then classified by topic in order to determine what type of events led to job satisfaction and job dissatisfaction.

The major finding of the study was that the events that led to satisfaction were of quite a different kind from those that led to dissatisfaction. Five factors stood out as strong determinants of job satisfaction: achievement, recognition, the attraction of the work itself, responsibility, and advancement. Lack of these five factors, though, was mentioned very infrequently in regard to job *dis*satisfaction. When the reasons for the dissatisfactions were analysed they were found to be concerned with a different range of factors: company policy and administration, supervision, salary, interpersonal relations and working conditions. Since such distinctly separate factors were found to be associated with job satisfaction and job dissatisfaction, Herzberg concludes that these two feelings are not the opposites of one another, rather they are concerned with two different ranges of man's needs.

The set of factors associated with job dissatisfaction are those stemming from man's overriding need to avoid physical and social deprivation. Using a biblical analogy, Herzberg relates these to the 'Adam' conception of the nature of man. When Adam was expelled from the Garden of Eden he was immediately faced with the task of satisfying the needs which stem from his animal nature; the needs for food, warmth, avoidance of pain, safety, security, belongingness, etc. Ever since then man has had to concern himself with the satisfaction of these needs together with those which, as a result of social conditioning, have been added to them. Thus, for example, man has learned that in certain economies the satisfaction of these needs makes it necessary to earn money which has therefore become a specific motivating drive.

In contrast, the factors associated with job satisfaction are those stemming from man's need to realize his human potential for perfection. In biblical terms this is the 'Abraham' conception of the nature of man. Abraham was created in the image of God. He was capable of great accomplishments, of development, of growth, of transcending his environmental limitations, of self-realization. Man has these aspects to his nature too, they are indeed the characteristically human ones. He has a need to understand, to achieve, and through achievement to experience psychological growth, and these needs are very powerful motivating drives.

Both the Adam and Abraham natures of man look for satisfaction in his work, but they do so in different ranges of factors. The Adam nature seeks the avoidance of dissatisfaction and is basically concerned with the job environment. It requires effective company policies, working conditions, security, pay, etc. and is affected by inadequacies in these. Since they are extrinsic to the job itself, Herzberg refers to them as 'job hygiene' or 'maintenance' factors. Just as lack of hygiene will cause disease, but the presence of hygienic conditions will not, of itself, produce health, so lack of adequate 'job hygiene' will cause dissatisfaction, but its presence will not of itself cause satisfaction. Satisfaction in work is provided through the Abraham nature of man which is concerned with the job content of the work itself, with achievement, recognition, responsibility, advancement, etc. These are the 'motivator' or growth factors and their presence will cause satisfaction. Their absence will not cause dissatisfaction (if the job hygiene factors are adequate) but will lead to an absence of positive satisfactions. It is thus basic to Herzberg's approach that job satisfaction and job dissatisfaction are not opposites, since they are concerned with different factors in work serving different aspects of the nature of man. The opposite of job satisfaction, therefore, is not job dissatisfaction but simply no job satisfaction. The opposite of job dissatisfaction, similarly, is lack of job dissatisfaction.

The finding of the original study – that the factors associated with job satisfaction were basically different in kind from those associated with job dissatisfaction – has been repeated in several subsequent studies. Collating the information based on twelve different investigations, involving over one thousand six hundred employees in a variety of jobs in business and other organizations and in a number of countries, Herzberg presents results to show that the overwhelming majority of the factors contributing to job satisfaction (81 per cent) were the motivators concerned with growth and development. A large majority of the factors contributing to job dissatisfaction (69 per cent) involved hygiene or environmental maintenance.

How, then, may this 'motivation–hygiene' approach be used to increase the motivation and job satisfaction of employees? First, it is clear that this cannot be done through the job hygiene factors. Certainly, these can and should be improved as they will reduce job dissatisfaction, but adequate company policies, working conditions, pay and supervision, are increasingly thought of as a right to be expected, not as an incentive to greater achievement and satisfaction. For this, the rewarding nature of the work itself, recognition, responsibility, opportunities for achievement and advancement are necessary. Herzberg recognizes that these are phrases that may be used nowadays in relation to jobs, but they are often used in a superficial way, or as inspirational talk without much effective action. He therefore advocates an industrial engineering approach, based on the design of jobs, but from the opposite point of view from that of Taylor (see p. 98). Instead of rationalizing and simplifying the work to increase efficiency, the motivation–hygiene theory suggests that jobs be enriched to include the motivating factors in order to bring about an effective utilization of people and to increase job satisfaction.

The principles of *job enrichment* require that the job be developed to include new aspects which provide the opportunity for the employee's psychological growth. It is important that the new aspects are capable of allowing this. Merely to add one undemanding job to another (as is often the case with job enlargement) or to switch from one undemanding job to another (as in job rotation) is not adequate. These are merely horizontal job loading. In contrast, job enrichment calls for vertical job loading, where opportunities for achievement, responsibility, recognition, growth and learning are designed into the job. The approach would be to look for ways of removing some controls while retaining or increasing an individual's accountability for his own work; giving a person a complete natural unit of work; granting additional authority to an employee in his job; increasing job freedom; making reports directly available to the man himself rather than to the supervisor; introducing new and more difficult tasks not previously undertaken, etc.

A number of experiments have been reported by Herzberg and his colleagues where these changes have been introduced with considerable effect. For example, in a study of the job of 'stockholder correspondent' of a large corporation the following suggestions were considered but rejected as involving merely horizontal job loading: firm fixed quotas could be set for letters to be answered each day, the employees could type the letters themselves as well as composing them, all difficult inquiries could be channelled to a few workers so that the rest could achieve high rates of output, the workers could be rotated through units handling different inquiries and then sent back to their own units. Instead, changes leading to the enrichment of jobs were introduced such as: correspondents were made directly responsible for the quality and accuracy of letters which were sent out directly over their own names (previously a verifier had checked all letters, the supervisor had rechecked and signed them and was responsible for their quality and accuracy), subject matter experts were appointed within each unit for other members to consult (previously the supervisor had dealt with all difficult and specialized questions), verification of experienced workers' letters was dropped from 100 per cent to 10 per cent and correspondents were encouraged to answer letters in a more personalized way instead of relying upon standard forms. In these ways, the jobs were enriched with resulting increases in both performance and job satisfaction.

In other studies, laboratory technicians ('experimental officers') were encouraged to write personal project reports in addition to those of the supervising scientists and were authorized to requisition materials and equipment direct; sales representatives were made wholly responsible for determining the calling frequencies on their customers and were given a discretionary range of about 10 per cent on the prices of most products; factory foremen were authorized to modify schedules, to hire labour against agreed manning targets, to appoint their deputies, and so on. In each case, the results in both performance and satisfaction were considerable.

The more subordinates' jobs become enriched, the more superfluous does 'on the job' supervision in the old sense become. But this does not downgrade the supervisors' job; in the companies studied they found themselves free to develop more important aspects of their jobs with a greater managerial component than they had had time to before. It soon becomes clear that supervising people who have authority of their own is a more demanding, rewarding and enjoyable task, than checking on every move of circumscribed automatons. For management the challenge is task organization to call out the motivators, and task support to provide adequate hygiene through company policy, technical supervision, working conditions, etc., thus satisfying both the Adam and the Abraham natures of man in work.

Bibliography

Work and the Nature of Man, World Publishing Co., 1966.
'One more time: How do you motivate employees?', *Harv. Bus. Rev.*, January – February 1968, pp. 53–62.

HERZBERG, F., MAUSNER, B., and SNYDERMAN, B., *The Motivation to Work*, Wiley, 1959.

PAUL, W. J. Jr, ROBERTSON, K. B., and HERZBERG, F., 'Job enrichment pays off', *Harv. Bus. Rev.*, March – April 1969, pp. 61–78.

Rensis Likert and Douglas McGregor

Rensis Likert is an American social psychologist. After war service as chief of the Morale Division of the United States Strategic Bombing Survey, he established in 1946 the Survey Research Center at the University of Michigan. In 1948 the Center was enlarged to become the Institute for Social Research with Likert as its first Director. He has thus been at the head of one of the major institutions conducting research into human behaviour in organizations. His book *New Patterns of Management* is a collation of research studies which he and his colleagues have conducted.

Douglas McGregor (1906–1964) was a social psychologist who published a number of research papers in this field. For some years he was President (i.e. chief executive) of Antioch College and he has described how this period as a top administrator affected his views on organizational functioning. From 1954 until his death, he was Professor of Management at the Massachusetts Institute of Technology.

'Managers with the best records of performance in American business and government are in the process of pointing the way to an appreciably more effective system of management than now exists,' proclaims Likert. Research studies have shown that departments which are low in efficiency tend to be in the charge of supervisors who are 'job-centred'. That is, they 'tend to concentrate on keeping their subordinates busily engaged in going through a specified work cycle in a prescribed way and at a satisfactory rate as determined by time standards'. This attitude is clearly derived from that of Taylor (see p. 98) with its emphasis on breaking down the job into component parts, selecting and training people to do them, and exerting constant pressure to achieve output. The supervisor sees himself as getting the job done with the resources (which includes the people) at his disposal.

Supervisors with the best record of performance are found to focus their attention on the human aspects of their subordinates' problems, and on building effective work groups which are set high achievement goals. These supervisors are 'employee-centred'. They regard their jobs as dealing with human beings rather than with the work; they attempt to know them as individuals. They see their function as helping them to do the job efficiently. They exercise general rather than detailed supervision, and are more concerned with targets than methods. They allow maximum participation in decision-making. If high performance is to be obtained, a supervisor must not only be employee-centred but must also have high performance goals and be capable of exercising the decision-making processes to achieve them.

In summarizing these findings, Likert distinguishes four systems of management. System 1 is the exploitive authoritative type where management uses fear and threats, communication is downward, superiors and subordinates are psychologically far apart, the bulk of decisions is taken at the top of the organization, etc. System 2 is the benevolent authoritative type where management uses rewards, attitudes are subservient to superiors, information flowing upward is restricted to what the boss wants to hear, policy decisions are taken at the top but decisions within a prescribed framework may be delegated to lower levels, etc. System 3 is the consultative type where management uses rewards, occasional punishments and some involvement is sought, communication is both down and up but upward communication other than that which the boss wants to hear is given in limited amounts and only cautiously, although subordinates can have a moderate amount of influence on the activities of their departments as broad policy decisions are taken at the top and more specific decisions at lower levels, etc.

System 4 is characterized by participative group management. Management give economic rewards and make full use of group participation and involvement in setting high performance goals, improving work methods, etc; communication flows downwards, upwards and with peers and is accurate; subordinates and superiors are very close psychologically. Decision-making is widely done throughout the organization through group processes, and is integrated into the formal structure by regarding the organization chart as a series of overlapping groups with each group linked to the rest of the organization by means of persons (called 'linking pins') who are members of more than one group. System 4 management produces high productivity, greater involvement of individuals, and better labour-management relations.

In general high-producing managers are those who have built the personnel in their units into effective groups, whose members have cooperative attitudes and a high level of job satisfaction through System 4 management. But there are exceptions. Technically competent, job-centred, tough management can achieve high productivity (particularly if backed up by tight systems of control techniques). But the members of units whose supervisors use these high-pressure methods are likely to have unfavourable attitudes towards their work and the management, and to have excessively high levels of waste and scrap. They also show higher labour turnover, and greater labour–management conflict as measured by work-stoppages, official grievances and the like.

Management, according to Likert, is always a relative process. To be effective and to communicate, a leader must always adapt his behaviour to take account of the *persons* whom he leads. There are no specific rules which will work well in all situations, but only general principles which must be interpreted to take account of the expectations, values and skills of those with whom the manager interacts. Sensitivity to these values and expectations is a crucial leadership skill, and organizations must create the atmosphere and conditions which encourage every manager to deal with the people he encounters in a manner fitting to their values and their expectations.

To assist in this task, management now has available a number of measures of relevant factors which have been developed by social scientists. Methods are available to obtain objective measurements of such variables as: the amount of member loyalty to an organization; the extent to which the goals of groups and individuals facilitate the achievement of the organization's goals; the level of motivation among members; the degree of confidence and trust between different hierarchical levels and between different sub-units; the efficiency and adequacy of the communication process; the extent to which each superior is correctly informed of the expectations, reactions, obstacles, problems and failures of his subordinates – together with the assistance they find useful and the assurance they wish they could get.

These measures and others enable an organization to know at any time the state of the system of functioning human beings which underpins it (called the 'interaction-influence system'); whether it is improving or deteriorating and why, and what to do to bring about desired improvements. This objective information about the interaction-influence system enables problems of leadership and management to be depersonalized and the 'authority of facts' to come to the fore. In this way the 'law of the situation' as Mary Parker Follett (see p. 104) called it, will determine which actions need to be taken. Likert states that the law of the situation can be used with far greater power today than when Follett proposed it. A much wider range of human behaviour can now be measured and made objective, whereas previously impressions and judgements had to suffice.

Douglas McGregor examines the assumptions about human behaviour which underlie managerial action. The traditional conception of administration (as exemplified by the writings of Fayol, pp. 60–65) is based upon the direction and control by management of the enterprise and its individual members. It implies certain basic assumptions about human motivation, which McGregor characterizes as 'Theory X'. These are:

1. 'The average human being has an inherent dislike of work and will avoid it if he can.' Thus management needs to stress

productivity, incentive schemes and 'a fair day's work'; and to denounce 'restriction of output'.

2. 'Because of this human characteristic of dislike of work, most people must be coerced, controlled, directed, threatened with punishment to get them to put forth adequate effort toward the achievement of organizational objectives.'

3. 'The average human being prefers to be directed, wishes to avoid responsibility, has relatively little ambition, wants security above all.'

Theory X has persisted for a long time (although it is not usually stated as baldly as this). It has done so because it has undoubtedly provided an explanation for *some* human behaviour in organizations. There are, however, many readily observable facts and a growing body of research findings (such as those described by Likert) which cannot be explained on these assumptions. McGregor proposes an alternative 'Theory Y', with the underlying principle of 'integration' to replace direction and control. The assumptions about human motivation of Theory Y are:

1. 'The expenditure of physical and mental effort in work is as natural as play or rest.' The ordinary person does not inherently dislike work: according to the conditions it may be a source of satisfaction or punishment.

2. External control is not the only means for obtaining effort. 'Man will exercise self-direction and self-control in the service of objectives to which he is committed.'

3. The most significant reward that can be offered in order to obtain commitment is the satisfaction of the individual's self-actualizing needs (compare Argyris, see p. 135). This can be a direct product of effort directed towards organizational objectives.

4. 'The average human being learns, under proper conditions, not only to accept but to seek responsibility.'

5. Many more people are able to contribute creatively to the solution of organizational problems than do so.

6. At present the potentialities of the average person are not being fully used.

McGregor develops an analysis of how the acceptance of Theory Y as the basis for running organizations would work out. He is particularly concerned with effects on performance appraisals, salaries and promotions, participation and staff–line relationships. On this last topic he makes the important point that there will be tension and conflict between staff and line as long as the staff departments are used as a service to top management to *control* the line (which is required by Theory X). With Theory Y the role of the staff is regarded as that of providing professional help to *all levels* of management.

The essential concept which both Likert and McGregor are propounding is that modern organizations, to be effective, must regard themselves as interacting groups of people with '*supportive relationships*' to each other. In the ideal, each member of the organization will feel that its objectives are of significance to him, that his job is meaningful, indispensable and difficult, that to do it effectively he needs and obtains support from his superiors – who regard the giving of this support to make *him* effective as their prime function.

Bibliography

McGREGOR, D., *The Human Side of Enterprise*, McGraw-Hill, 1960.

LIKERT, R., *New Patterns of Management*, McGraw-Hill, 1961.

McGREGOR, D., *Leadership and Motivation*, MIT Press, 1966.

LIKERT, R., *The Human Organization: Its Management and Value*, McGraw-Hill, 1967.

McGREGOR, D., *The Professional Manager*, McGraw-Hill, 1967.

Robert R. Blake and Jane S. Mouton

Robert Blake and Jane Mouton are respectively President and Vice-President of Scientific Methods, Inc., an organization which provides behavioural science consultancy services to industry. Both are psychologists, trained in American universities. Blake first designed and tested the 'Managerial Grid' during his subsequent employment in manufacturing industry.

Blake and Mouton start from the assumption that a manager's job is to foster attitudes and behaviour which promote efficient performance, stimulate and use creativity, generate enthusiasm for experimentation and innovation, and learn from interaction with others. Such managerial competence can be taught and it can be learned. Their managerial grid provides a framework for understanding and applying effective management.

The grid sets the guidelines for an approach to management which has been widely applied. It has been successful in North America, in Europe, and in Asia; in production work, sales, and R. & D., in trade unions, and in military, government, and welfare organizations. Its relevance appears to transcend cultural boundaries and forms of organization. Moreover, it has been applied from supervisory jobs to executive levels.

The managerial grid results from combining two fundamental ingredients of managerial behaviour. One is concern for production: the other is concern for people. 'Concern for' does not mean a dedication to specific targets, nor does it mean the results achieved in themselves. It means the general approach to management which governs the actions of a supervisor or manager, just *how* he concerns himself with production and with people.

Concern for production does not mean only physical factory products. The term production can refer to the number of good research ideas, the number of accounts processed, the volume of sales, the quality of service given or of top policy decisions made, and so on. Concern for people similarly includes all of concern for friendships, for personal commitment to tasks, for someone's self-respect, for equitable payment, and so on.

Any manager's approach to management will show more or less of each of these two fundamental constituents. A manager may show a high degree of production concern together with low people concern, or the other way around. Or he may be middling on both. Indeed all of these are commonplace and it is also commonplace that none of these is satisfactory. Placing the two fundamentals as the axes of a graph enables a grid to be drawn which reveals very simply not only many typical combinations seen in the behaviour of managers every day, but also the desirable combination of 'concerns for' as follows:

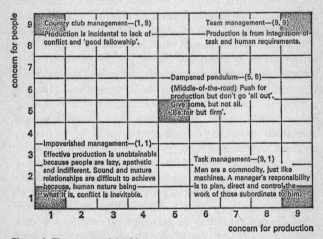

Figure 1 The managerial grid

(From Blake and Mouton, 'The managerial grid', *Advanced Management Office Executive*, 1962, vol. 1 no. 9

Different positions on the grid represent different typical patterns of behaviour. The grid suggests that change should be towards *both* high concern for people (scores 9) and high concern for production (also scores 9) simultaneously, that is, to a 9,9 managerial style of 'team management'.

The grid indicates that all degrees of concern for production and concern for people are possible; but for simplicity five styles of management are picked out for illustration.

9,1 management, or 'task management', focuses overwhelmingly on production. A 9,1 manager is an exacting task master who expects schedules to be met and people to do what they are told, no more and no less. Anything that goes wrong will be viewed as due to someone's mistake, and that someone must be found and the blame squarely placed. Supervisors make decisions. Subordinates carry them out. The manager should run his own show, and disagreement is likely to be viewed as the next thing to insubordination. 9,1 management can achieve high production, at least in the short run, but it has a number of deficiencies. Any creative energies of subordinates go into how to defeat the system rather than how to improve it. Disagreements are ruled out and suppressed rather than settled. Subordinates do what is required, but no more, and seem 'obviously' indifferent and apathetic. Win-lose thinking is eventually reflected in the development of trade unions and struggles between unions and managements. 9,1 management is prevalent in a competitive industrial society such as the USA because inadequate education leaves many people unable to use more than limited skills and compelled to endure this kind of supervision.

The 1,9 managerial style, or 'country club management' as it has been called, emphasizes solely concern for people. It does not push people for production because 'you can lead a horse to water, but you can't make him drink'. People are encouraged and supported, and their mistakes are overlooked because they are doing the best they can. The key word is togetherness (W. H. Whyte, p. 165) and informal conversation, coffee together, and a joke help things along. The informal rule is 'no work discussions during breaks'. But country club management also has deficiencies. People try to avoid direct disagreements or criticisms of one another and production problems are glossed over. No one should be upset even if work is not going quite as it should. New ideas which might cause trouble or objectives which would cause strain are let slide. The 1,9 style easily grows up in quasi-monopoly situations or when operating on a cost-plus basis: and its ultimate end may be the complete closing of a non-competitive unit.

Little concern for either production or people results in 'impoverished management', the 1,1 style. It is difficult to imagine a whole organization surviving for long with this kind of management, but it is frequent enough in individual managers and supervisors. 1,1 management is characterized by the avoidance of responsibility or personal commitment. The supervisor leaves people to work as they think fit. He does just enough so that if anything goes wrong he can say 'I told them what to do – it's not my problem.' He minimizes contacts with anyone and is non-committal on any problems which come to him. The 1,1 approach typically reveals the frustration of someone who has been passed over for promotion, shunted sideways, or has been for years in a routine job (as Argyris, p. 136 also suggests).

Managers frequently alternate between the 1,9 'country club' style and the 9,1 'task management' style. They tighten up to increase output, 9,1 style, but when human relationships begin to suffer the pendulum swings right across to 1,9 again. The middle of the managerial grid shows the 5,5 'dampened pendulum' style, typified by marginal shifts around the happy medium. This middle-of-the-road style pushes enough to get acceptable production but yields enough to maintain acceptable morale. To aim fully for both is too idealistic. The manager aims at a moderate carrot and stick standard, fair but firm, and has confidence in his subordinate's ability to meet targets. 5,5 management thus gives rise to 'splitting the difference' on problems, to attempting balanced solutions rather than appropriate ones.

Unlike 5,5 management, and all the other styles, 9,9 'team

management' shows high concern for production and high concern for people, and does not accept that these concerns are incompatible. The team manager seeks to integrate people around production. Morale is task-related. Unlike 5,5, the 9,9 style tries to discover the best and most effective solutions, and aims at the highest attainable production to which all involved contribute and in which everyone finds his own sense of accomplishment. People satisfy their own needs through the job and working with others, not through incidental sociability in the 'country club style'. The 9,9 manager assumes that employees who know what the stakes are for them and others in what they are doing will not need boss direction and control (as Likert, p. 146). The manager's responsibility is to see to it that work is planned and organized by those with a stake in it and not necessarily by himself. Objectives should be clear to all, and though demanding should be realistic. It is accepted that conflict will occur, but problems are confronted directly and openly and not as personal disputes. This encourages creativity. Sustained improvement of the form of organization and development of those in it are both aims and likely outcomes of a 9,9 style.

9,9 management implicitly assumes a certain approach to conflict, both individual and between groups such as departments, headquarters office and field staff, labour and management, or the managements of newly merged corporations. In their book *Managing Intergroup Conflict*, Blake and Mouton together with Herbert Shepherd examine common reactions to such conflict and again suggest a style or approach which may lead to better solutions.

Many managers assume that conflicts are inevitable and cannot be resolved as such. If A and B disagree, then the result must favour one or the other. There may be a win–lose power struggle; or reference to a third party (e.g. overall boss) for a decision; or a stalemate which leaves the conflict unresolved until something happens which settles it or removes it, i.e. 'fate arbitration'. A second kind of assumption is that conflict can be avoided since groups need not be interdependent and can get on with things separately. Under this approach, one party to a disagreement gives up and withdraws; or both parties isolate themselves from the other; or everyone concerned puts on a façade of indifference. Third, managers can assume that agreement *is* possible. This can lead to an effort to preserve harmony by stressing common interests – though the real issues of disagreement remain; or some compromise may be achieved, perhaps through a bargaining approach to mutual accommodation; or a genuine effort can be made to find a positive resolution of points of difference.

Of the nine responses to conflict that have been summarized, this last problem-solving is the only one that does not leave the problems themselves still in being to greater or lesser degree. It requires a special kind of optimistic view of the capacities of other groups as well as one's own in facing whatever the problems may be.

Blake and Mouton advocate a systematically phased programme of organizational development which will move the style of management in an organization towards a 9,9 concern with production and people, and a problem-solving approach to conflict. In Phase 1 the Managerial Grid is studied as a framework for understanding organizational behaviour through off-site training. Phase 2 focuses on the on-site training in problem-solving methods of actual functioning teams as a whole. The same kind of application is made in Phase 3 but to inter-group work between units of the company where cooperation and coordination are necessary. Phase 4 is concerned with setting group goals for the optimum performance of the total organization. In Phase 5 the resulting changes are implemented, and Phase 6 measures these changes in order to consolidate them and set new goals for the future. Where evaluation of this programme has been carried out (see Blake *et al.*, 1964) the evidence points to more successful organizations and to greater career accomplishments by individual managers, as its results.

5 The Organization in Society

What is occurring . . . is a drive for social dominance, for power and privilege, for the position of ruling class, by the social group or class of the managers.

James Burnham

We do need to know how to cooperate with The Organization but, more than ever, so do we need to know how to resist it.

William H. Whyte

An organization so often ends by smothering the very thing which it was created to embody.

Kenneth Boulding

The danger to liberty lies in the subordination of belief to the needs of the industrial system.

J. K. Galbraith

Organizations do not exist or operate in a vacuum. They are one sort of institution in a particular society. They have to conform to the needs and standards laid down by institutions other than themselves. The pressures of a market economy, political decisions, legal restrictions, all affect organizational operations. Yet the large-scale organization is one of the dominant institutions of our time, and in its turn must exert a powerful influence on the rest of society. Many writers have taken up this theme and have tried to show how far the nature of modern organizations has changed society.

James Burnham develops the argument that the balance of power in society has shifted from the owners of wealth to those who manage it, to a point that constitutes a revolution. This led to the rise of a completely new group – the managerial class. For William H. Whyte also, managers are an increasingly assertive section of society, and he is alarmed that their characters are being moulded by the organization which employs them. Kenneth Boulding describes the conflicts organizations create in the loyalties of their members, and the conflicts between the interests of organizations and the wider interests of society. J. K. Galbraith suggests that these conflicts underline the inadequacy of the market mechanism for regulating economies, and points to the increasingly frequent intervention of governments as a 'countervailing power'.

James Burnham

James Burnham was born in 1905. He went to the University of Princeton and to Balliol College, Oxford, and from 1932 to 1954 was Professor of Philosophy at New York University. In 1955 he became editor of the *National Review*. During the thirties he was a member of the Trotskyite 'Fourth International', but he broke his Marxist connection in 1939. His many publications are mainly on political topics.

The term 'managerial revolution' has become part of the language since Burnham made it the title of his best-known book, written in 1940. As he himself points out, his views are not all that original, but they do constitute an attempt to formulate and argue logically about certain ideas which many people have wondered about, both then and since.

Burnham's thesis is that a declining capitalist form of society is giving way not to Marxist socialism, as is often suggested, but to a 'managerial society'. The managerial revolution by which this is being accomplished is not a violent upheaval but rather a transition over a period of time, in much the same way as feudal society gave way to capitalism. A wide range of symptoms heralded the imminent demise of capitalism as the Second World War commenced. The capitalist nations were unable to cope with mass unemployment, with permanent agricultural depression, and with the rapid rise in public and private debt. Their major ideologies of individualism, 'natural rights' of property, and private initiative were no longer accepted by the mass of the people.

But there is no reason to think that socialism is the inevitable consequence. Almost everywhere the Marxist parties are insignificant as a political force. The working class is declining in relative size and power. In Russia, the abolition of private property rights, which in Marxist theory should bring a classless socialist society, has neither prevented a ruling class from emerging nor promoted workers' control. Nevertheless, 'though Russia did not move toward socialism at the same time it did not move back to capitalism'. What happened in Russia, as is steadily happening throughout the world, was a movement towards a managerial type of society. In this society it will be the managers who are dominant, who have power and privilege, who have control over the means of production, and have preference in the distribution of rewards. In short, the managers will be the ruling class. This does not necessarily mean that the political offices will be occupied by managers, any more than under capitalism all politicians were capitalists, but that the real power over what is done will be in the hands of managers.

In order to define who the managers are, Burnham singles out four groups of people with different functions. There are stockholders, whose relationship to a company is entirely passive. There are financiers – capitalists whose interest is the financial aspects of numbers of companies irrespective of what those companies do. There are executives who guide a company, watch its profits and its prices. There are those who have charge of the technical process of producing, who organize men, materials and equipment, who develop the know-how which is becoming increasingly indispensable. These last are the managers. Of the stockholders, financiers, executives and managers, only the managers are vital to the process of production. This has been demonstrated by state ownership in Russia, and by the extension of state enterprise in other nations. Moreover, even where private owners continue, they have been getting farther and farther away from the instruments of production, delegating supervision of production to others, exercising control at second, third or fourth hand through financial devices.

Burnham remarks on the self-confidence of managers compared with bankers, owners, workers, farmers and shopkeepers. These latter display doubts and worries, but managers have a self-assurance founded on the strength of their position.

In managerial society there is no sharp distinction between politics and the arena of economics. In the state commissions, the committees, the bureaux, the administrative agencies, managers and bureaucrats coalesce. Rules, regulations and laws come increasingly to be issued by these interconnected bodies. The law is to be found in their records rather than in the annals of parliament. So in many nations sovereignty is gradually shifting from parliament to the administrative offices.

In such an economy the managers will exercise power by occupying the key directing positions. But their preferential rewards will be less in wealth and property rights than in status in the political–economic structure.

Burnham also sees the outlines of the managerial ideologies which will replace the individualistic capitalist ideologies. The stress will be on the state, the people, the race; on planning rather than freedom, jobs rather than opportunity, duties and order rather than natural right.

Burnham's analysis of the overall trends in society and his projection of these into the future arouse interest to the extent that events bear him out. He was writing as the Second World War began. Much that has happened since could be construed, either way, for or against his arguments. Years later, W. H. Whyte's description of The Organization and Organization Man is in keeping with Burnham's forecast. Is there a managerial revolution?

Bibliography
The Managerial Revolution, Peter Smith, 1941.

William H. Whyte

The American writer William H. Whyte is a journalist, and a student of the society in which he lives. He was born in 1917, and graduated in English at Princeton University in 1939. He has been on the staff of *Fortune* and has published articles in this and other leading magazines.

Whyte has concerned himself with contemporary trends in American society, and his book *The Organization Man* is an attempt to portray vividly one such trend which Whyte himself feels can go too far. He points to the coming of an organization man who not only works for The Organization but belongs to it as well. Such a man is a member of the middle class who occupy the middle rankings in all the great self-perpetuating institutions. Few of these ever become top managers, but they have 'taken the vows of organization life' and committed themselves to it.

Whyte argues that for an organization man of this kind the traditional Protestant ethic is becoming too distant from reality to provide an acceptable creed. The Protestant ethic is summed up by Whyte as the system of beliefs in the virtues of thrift, hard work and independence, and in the sacredness of property and the enervating effect of security. It extols free competition between individuals in the struggle for wealth and success. But to Whyte life is no longer like this, if it ever was. To him 'that upward path toward the rainbow of achievement leads smack through the conference room'. The younger generation of management have begun to recognize themselves as bureaucrats, even if they cannot face the word itself and prefer to describe themselves as administrators.

Such people need a different faith to give meaning to what they do, and Whyte finds in American society a gradually emerging body of thought to meet the need. He calls it the *social ethic*. This ethic provides the moral justification for the pressures of society against the individual. It holds that the individual is meaningless by himself, but that by being absorbed into the group he can create a whole that is greater than the sum of its parts. There should be no conflicts between man and society; any that occur are misunderstandings which can be prevented by better human relations.

There are three major propositions in the social ethic: *scientism, belongingness* and *togetherness*. Scientism, as Whyte dubs it, is the belief that a science of man can be created in the same way as the physical sciences were developed. If only there were enough time and money, the conditions apposite to good group dynamics or to personal adjustment to social situations or any other desired human response could be discovered. Believers in scientism (who are not to be confused with social scientists) could then generate the belongingness and togetherness which they seek for all. The ultimate need of man, it is thought, is to belong to a group, to harmonize himself with a group. But man needs togetherness in belonging. He wants not merely to be a part of The Organization but to immerse himself in it together with other people, in smaller groups around the conference table, in the seminar, the discussion group, the project team and so on.

Whyte traces the career cycle of organization man as, guided by his social ethic, he gives himself up to The Organization. The influence of The Organization has extended into college curricula, and by the time students are looking for their first job they have already turned their backs on the Protestant ethic. They look for a life of calm and order, offering success but not too much success, money but not too much, advancement but not too far. The Organization attempts to recruit for itself those who will fit in, those who will get along well with others, those who will not have any disturbingly exceptional characteristics. Increasingly it uses the tools of the psychologist: not only the well-tried aptitude and intelligence tests but tests purporting to reveal personality. Whyte challenges the validity of these latter tests, and goes so far as to write an

Appendix entitled 'How to Cheat on Personality Tests'. To obtain a safe personality score, you should try to answer as if you were like everybody else is supposed to be.

Once recruited, the training of the potential manager emphasizes not his own work but the exploitation of human relations techniques to manage the work of others. The successful trainee is not the one who competes successfully with the others but the one who cooperates more than the others cooperate. What of the loss of individualism in group life? Young men today, says Whyte, regard this aspect of the large organization as a positive boon. Their ideal is 'the well-rounded man'. Such a man has time for family and hobbies. He is good on the job but not too zealous or over-involved in it: overwork may have been necessary in the past but now The Organization looks for 'the full man'. In particular, this is the image held by the personnel manager and the business school.

The same tendencies Whyte also sees in scientific and academic institutions. The idea of the lone genius is being displaced by that of the group-conscious research team. There is a steady increase in the proportion of scientific papers by several authors compared with those by a single author.

Though Whyte is stating a case against too great a belief in the social ethic, he realistically points out that it may never be applied as absolutely as it is preached, any more than was the Protestant ethic. Even so, the social ethic may delude the individual that his interests are being cared for when The Organization is really following its own ends. Guided by it, The Organization may suppress individual imagination, and may cling to a mediocre consensus. People may become skilful in getting along with one another yet fail to ask why they should get along; may strive for adjustment, but fail to ask to what they are adjusting. It is Whyte's contention that organization man must fight The Organization, and accept conflict between himself and society.

However, for some few in The Organization who start to go ahead of their contemporaries there comes a realization that they have committed themselves: that they must go on alone to higher executive positions, that their home lives will be shortened and their wives less and less interested in the struggle. Such men find themselves working fifty- and sixty-hour weeks; taking work home; spending week-ends at conferences. They have not time for anything else. More than this, their work is their self-expression and they do not want anything else. They discover that the man on his way to the top cannot be 'well-rounded'. The dream of a comfortable contentment just short of the top is shattered, and they talk of the treadmill, the merry-go-round, and the rat race, 'words that convey an absence of tangible goals but plenty of activity to get there'.

So the executive contains within himself the conflict between the old Protestant ethic and the new social ethic. The man who goes ahead does so to control his own destiny; yet in The Organization he must be controlled *and* look as if he likes it. Even though he wants to be dominant, he must applaud permissive management. He has risen by being a good team player but now more and more he sees the other side – the frustration of the committee, the boredom of being sociable. Here is the executive's neurosis.

Bibliography

The Organization Man, Simon & Schuster, 1956; Penguin, 1960.

Kenneth E. Boulding

Kenneth Boulding was born in England and educated at Oxford. He has held a variety of teaching posts at universities in Scotland, Canada and the United States, and is now Professor of Economics in the University of Michigan. He is the author of many books on economics, but his work on *The Organizational Revolution* springs from his interest in the relationship between organizations and ethical systems.

Boulding sees this 'revolution' as one of the major events of the past hundred years. There has been a great rise in the number, size and power of all organizations. More and more spheres of activity have become organized so that there are now businesses, trade unions, employers' federations, political parties, farming groups, the state, all of which are highly organized. This revolution is due on the one hand to changes in the habits and needs of people and on the other to changes in the skills and techniques of organizing. Boulding sees the latter as the more important. Henry Ford did not mass-produce motor-cars because of the demand but because of new knowledge on how to organize and make them. Supply, not demand, was the dominant factor.

Such a growth of organizations has given rise to a large number of ethical problems. In Western societies there are certain basic values and assumptions which are drawn from Christianity. The Ten Commandments and the Sermon on the Mount are still largely the final basis for an ethical analysis of behaviour. They define morality as a matter of personal relationships, with a Christian ideal of fellowship and equality. It is on the level of personal behaviour that the application of such principles gives rise to ethical problems in organizations.

All organizations create an 'in-group' made up of members of the organization, and an 'out-group' of non-members. The moral dilemma for the individual in such a situation is that the defence of the inner fellowship necessarily means the breaking of wider fellowships. To whom does the individual owe his moral allegiance?

As organizations grow larger and more powerful there is an increased pressure for a hierarchy to fix the relationships and distribution of power between people. But the presence of such a hierarchy is directly in conflict with the moral idea of equality. It tends to produce an aristocratic, highly stratified society based on status. Political democracy is an attempt to overcome this moral dilemma, making the people at the top dependent on the will of the people.

The ideals of Christianity are also what Boulding calls 'familistic'. A full and intimate relationship of love and concern is the ideal human relationship. The major virtue is love, and the closest one gets to this is in the family. Such an ideal constantly comes into conflict with the necessities of organizational life. Relationships in economic organizations are based on contract which demands only a lesser virtue, that of integrity. For large-scale organizations to exist, relationships must be pared down to the minimum, losing something vital as a consequence. The special moral problem of the businessman is balancing the equation of love and necessity. 'The business world is one in which relationships are based mainly on faith and hope, and, if it seems to be deficient in the warmer virtue of charity, it must at least be given credit for the other two.'

However, ethical problems also arise for organizations at levels other than that of personal relationships. To what extent should the leaders of any organization feel a responsibility to society as a whole? Should they advocate policies for the whole society rather than for their own special interests? What are the obligations of an organization to society? Boulding says that the usual excuse for pursuing special interests is that one is acting as a counter-pressure against other interests. The menace to society lies in the fact that certain special interests may become powerful enough to demand, and receive, privileged protection.

The heart of ethical conduct is action in the general interest. The problem is to make sure that organizations acting in such a way survive, and that those not meeting the needs and ends of society disappear. But this must be done without the use of coercion, which is inimical to the pursuit of Christian ideals. Action in the general interest is an ideal which is difficult to attain and the need is for a mechanism which will continually adjust actual to ideal.

The mechanism to achieve this is the market reacting to the laws of supply and demand. Competition and specialization which are the mainsprings of a market economy are prime movers in bringing together the general interest with special interests. But the organizational revolution has superimposed monoplies and large-scale economic groupings on the market economy. So the need is for a *governed* market economy with the principle of political representation built into it which makes an individual responsible to others for his actions. There has been a shift from the market to representation as the adjustive mechanism. It is through the operation of social democracy that the best approximation of the ideal and the actual can be made.

Bibliography
The Organizational Revolution, Harper & Row, 1953.

John K. Galbraith

J. K. Galbraith was born in Canada, but has lived most of his life in the USA. He is an economist who has spent his academic years at Harvard University. He was a supporter of John Kennedy and during the Kennedy administration served as US Ambassador to India. Galbraith has long believed in the necessity of popularizing the ideas of economics, and his books are as much aimed at the layman as the professional economist.

His underlying thesis in all his work is that American capitalism has changed its nature over the past fifty years, and as a result, traditional economic theories no longer apply. Classical economic theory rests on the proposition that the behaviour of buyers and sellers is regulated by the market, through which the stimulant of competition is provided. Economic power is denied to any one person or firm because of price competition. But this system depends on a large number of producers of a good or service, none of whom is in a position to dominate the market; conversely it depends on large numbers of buyers, who individually cannot affect the market. Yet this is demonstrably not the situation in modern industrial economies. Instead there is a process by which the typical industry passes from an initial stage of many firms competing, to a situation of a few large firms only, i.e. what economists refer to as oligopoly.

Thus, the most important task facing modern economic theory is to analyse the place of the large corporation in the economy, and to discover what, if any, new regulatory agencies have replaced the marketplace. If the balanced power of the competitive system no longer applies, does the large corporation wield unchecked power? In *American Capitalism*,

Galbraith suggests that there is a situation of countervailing power. The concentration of industrial enterprise, on which everyone agrees, produces the giant corporations which might possibly produce huge agglomerations of power both in economic and political terms. But this process brings into existence strong buyers as well as strong sellers. This is something that tends to be forgotten when the supposed 'evils' of oligopoly are discussed. An example of such countervailing power is seen in the development of large retail trading chains, such as Marks & Spencer and the Co-operative Movement, who from their importance as buyers of goods are able to offset the oligopoly power of the producers or sellers of shirts, dresses, etc. Similarly, in the labour market there is the power of the union countervailing that of the employers' association. Thus, the situation is one of giants standing off against each other. Much of the increasing intervention in the economy by the state comes from the need to develop sources of countervailing power in the economy. A recent phenomenon in the USA and Britain which fits the theory is the development of vocal consumers' associations.

So, the competitive marketplace as regulator is replaced, due to the differences between the capitalistic system of today and that of fifty years ago. And such a system has its efficiencies. It is the large oligopolies which can best incur the cost of research. However, Galbraith himself points out that this system of countervailing power really only works where there is limited demand, so that the buyer has some leeway *vis-à-vis* the seller. In the context of unlimited demand the balance of power shifts decisively to the seller, the large corporation. And in *The Affluent Society* and *The New Industrial State* he develops the idea of control of the market by the corporation, where a situation of unlimited demand is 'manufactured'.

Again the starting idea is the rise of the large scale corporation and separation of ownership from control and the results of this for a competitive market system (see Burnham, p. 161). Control of the market becomes increasingly important for the well-being of the organization because of the use of more and more sophisticated technology. The organization faces a set of technological imperatives (technology being the systematic application of scientific or other organized knowledge to practical tasks). For Galbraith there are six imperatives deriving from increased technological sophistication which have important implications for the relationship of the organization to other organizations, to the consumer, and to the state.

First, the time span between thinking of a new product and actually producing it is getting greater and greater. An example is the lead time between the initial idea for the Mini car and its arrival on the market. Secondly, the amount of capital that is committed to production increases; more investment is required. Thirdly, once time and money have been committed there is a great deal of inflexibility; it becomes very difficult to back out. Fourthly, the use of advanced technology requires special sorts of manpower and we have the rise of the engineer, the applied scientist, the importance of technical qualifications. (As with Burnham, Galbraith sees this 'technostructure' becoming the important source of decision-making.) Fifthly, organizations become more complex, with an increasing need for the control and coordination of the specialists. Sixthly, all these imperatives together produce the need for planning.

Thus, societies require large corporations (which Galbraith names The Industrial System, the dominant feature of the New Industrial State) properly to acquire the benefits of new technology. But it is obvious that the imperatives outlined above involve the organization in situations of risk. There are always the famous cases of the Ford Edsel and the Rolls-Royce aero-engines as salutory reminders of what can happen when planning fails. It is only the large business organization which can find the necessary capital and employ the necessary skills to use sophisticated technology, but it still needs help in dealing with this, and with the risks involved.

Organizational planning does not just mean making sure that the right materials get to the right place at the right time, internally. It also means that suppliers are reliable, producing goods, components, etc., as needed, and that the buyers are there when needed. As a result, to quote Galbraith: 'Much of what the firm regards as planning consists in minimizing or getting rid of market influences.' To deal with the uncertainties involved, and thus minimize the risks facing the organization, planning is required to *replace the market*. Control of the market can be done in two ways: either by direct control of the consumer, making him dependent in some way on the corporation, or by having a single customer – a guaranteed market. Both of these options involve increasing state intervention, another illustration of the changing nature of contemporary capitalism.

Direct control of the consumer can take place in a variety of ways. One of the most important is the use of advertising. This is a direct attempt to influence the demand for a product and also to create a psychological dependence on the part of the consumer. Under conditions of affluence a situation of unlimited demand can be created with the corporation controlling the needs and aspirations of the consumer rather than vice versa. In the USA the accepted view of a desirable automobile is the current model as styled in and by Detroit. A further possibility is the control of the market by size domination, a movement towards monopoly. This can be helped along by vertical integration and the use of contracts to tie buyers and sellers together, stabilizing the existence of both. The state is important in that it now carries the responsibility for regulating the level of demand in the economy, stabilizing wages and prices.

Having a single customer guaranteed market becomes extremely important for those organizations having especially advanced, expensive technologies. In particular what happens is that the state becomes the customer and the idea of a market starts to disappear altogether. The state is in effect underwriting the cost of investment, and the line between the 'private' corporation and the state begins to disappear. This situation is typical of the aerospace industry, where research, development and production are commissioned by the government. An organization such as Lockheed sells more than three-quarters of its production to the government.

With the need to control demand, and the role of the state in this process, there is a tendency for the corporation to become a part of the administrative arm of the state. The management of demand becomes a vast, rapidly growing industry in which the public sector is increasingly important through its control of the wage-price spiral, its control of personal and corporate income tax, its regulation of aggregate demand, and its own role as a consumer. Also, the state is responsible for producing the qualified manpower (the technostructure) on which the corporation is dependent, through its financing of education.

The net result is an increasing similarity between all mature industrial societies in terms of the design of organizations and the planning mechanisms used. The heavy requirements of capital, sophisticated technology and elaborate organization which need planning to replace the market, lead to the dominance of the large corporation. And such corporations are dependent on the state. As Galbraith summarizes his position: 'Given the decision to have modern industry (in any country), much of what happens is inevitable and the same.'

Bibliography

The Affluent Society, Hamish Hamilton, 1958; Penguin, 1967.
American Capitalism, Houghton Mifflin, 1962; Penguin, 1963.
The New Industrial State, Houghton Mifflin, 1967; Penguin, 1969.